The Sunday School Board: *Ninety Years of Service*

Walter B. Shurden
James L. Sullivan

The
SUNDAY SCHOOL
BOARD
Ninety Years of Service

WALTER B. SHURDEN

BROADMAN PRESS
Nashville, Tennessee

Advisory Committee Who Contributed to This Book

Dessel Aderholt

Martin Bradley

Annie Ward Byrd

James Clark

Thomas Clark

Grady Cothen

Robert Fulbright

Johnnie Godwin

David Haywood

Reuben Herring

Lucy Hoskins

Lloyd Householder

John Jackson

Jack Jewell

Marian Keegan

Linda Lawson

Gomer Lesch

Melody McCoy

Maines Rawls

Jerry Ross

Charles Treadway

Ejay Vidrine

Donald Whitehouse

© Copyright 1981 • Broadman Press.

4265-58

ISBN: 0-8054-6558-8

Dewey Decimal Classification: 286.06

Subject heading: SUNDAY SCHOOL BOARD

Library of Congress Catalog Card Number: 80-68749

Printed in the United States of America

For
Findley Edge,
The Basil Manly Professor of Religious Education
at The Southern Baptist Theological Seminary
for thirty-three years,
and for
Louvenia Edge,
who has served with him in ministry
to students and churches of the Southern Baptist Convention

Frost (1891–1893, 1896–1916): Builder

Bell (1893–1896): Fighter

Van Ness (1916–1935): Educator

Holcomb (1935–1953): Pastor

Sullivan (1953–1975): Balancer

Broad Strokes that Characterize the Successors to the "Royal Line"

Cothen (1975–   ): Bible Promoter

Preface

In this brief history of The Sunday School Board of the Southern Baptist Convention, I have sought to "feel the pulse" of the institution in its ninety years of history. Details of institutional organization and statistics have been intentionally omitted. Also intentional, but far more unfortunate, has been the neglect of numerous personalities who have served in silence and who have deserved more of the ink than any history to this point has given them.

This is the fifth published history of the Board. J. M. Frost wrote the first in 1914. His is the most important for understanding the origins and early struggles of the institution simply because it was written by the founder and first executive of the Board. Frost awkwardly entitled his history, *The Sunday School Board, Southern Baptist Convention: Its History and Work.*

P. E. Burroughs, longtime employee of the Board, wrote the second and third accounts to celebrate the fortieth and fiftieth anniversaries of the Board. Published in 1931, the fortieth-anniversary history was *The Story of the Sunday School Board of the Southern Baptist Convention.* It is sketchy, without interpretation, and not of great value in understanding "the story." The fiftieth-anniversary history, *Fifty Fruitful Years, 1891-1941,* is extremely helpful, providing insights into the persons and circumstances which helped shape the Sunday School Board. Robert A. Baker, professor of church history at Southwestern Seminary, wrote *The Story of the Sunday School Board* to celebrate seventy-five years of the Board's history. It is the most comprehensive history of the institution to date.

Two other works, though not full-fledged histories of the Board, constitute valuable contributions for a study of the Board. One is Joe W. Burton's *Road to Nashville,* an account of the birth of the Board which highlights J. M. Frost. Unpublished but invaluable for a study of the Board is the work of Lynn E. May, Jr., and A. Ronald Tonks, both of the Historical Commission of the Southern Baptist Convention. They have compiled "A Resumé of Events in the Background and History of the Sunday School Board," which is a historian's delight.

I once asked Clyde Fant, Jr., to tell me in a sentence the most important aspect of preaching. After telling me that he could not tell me in just one sentence, he said, "You have to go for the life." He meant that you have "to go for the life" of the text and that you have "to go for the life" of the hearer.

Here I have tried "to go for the life" of the Board. I have wanted to discover the rhythm and the movement, the various moods of the Board as expressed under its six executives. To understand these moods, one has to know something about the people who have led the Board. One also has to know something about the social, cultural, and denominational context of the Board in each stage of its historical development. Therefore, I have tried, in the limited space available, to couch the story in both the personal and the social contexts. The various moods of the Board are clear to me. I hope they will be for you.

Three women helped me immensely. Marian Keegan assisted in research. Marcia Childers typed the manuscript. Kay Shurden proofread it and also directed me to my desk.

Contents

1 Manly, Broadus, and "a Royal Line"

Characteristic of so much of its future life, The Sunday School Board of the Southern Baptist Convention was born in denominational conflict. J. M. Frost, the father of the Board, described those early years as "days of storm and stress."[1] But in the midst of the storm, Southern Baptists organized the Sunday School Board in 1891.

In the first annual report of The Sunday School Board to the Southern Baptist Convention in 1892, Frost said, "In this report today we take up a broken thread in the history of the Southern Baptist Convention, reviewing a work begun and fostered more than twenty-five years ago by some of the best men God has ever given to the denomination."[2] What did Frost mean by "a broken thread"? And who were these "best men God has ever given to the denomination"? And what did he mean when he later wrote that the Sunday School Board stood in "a royal line"?

Frost was, of course, talking about heritage. The history of Southern Baptist efforts to establish a denominational publication and Sunday School enterprise was definitely "a broken thread." Actually, it was more like "broken threads." Not just once, but several times Southern Baptist efforts in this type of ministry were interrupted.

The first interruption occurred with the American Baptist Publication Society. Begun in Washington, D.C., in 1824, twenty one years before the formation of the Southern Baptist Convention, this national Baptist organization received solid support from the South. With the founding of the Southern

Baptist Convention in 1845, however, tension was placed on the relationship of Baptists of the South and the ABPS, which had been moved to Philadelphia in 1826. After 1845 some Southern Baptists did not want to be dependent on the Northern-based society. Tension became blatant rivalry. And eventually, after a half-century, the thread connecting Baptists of the South to the ABPS broke.

The second "broken thread" was the Southern Baptist Publication Society. Though never officially related to the SBC, this society signaled an early surge of sectionalism and denominationalism among Southern Baptists. When the slavery issue drove Southern Baptists to Augusta, Georgia, in 1845 to form their own convention, they intended their separation from the North to include only foreign and home missions. The SBC, therefore, organized only two Boards in 1845. One was the Foreign Mission Board, placed in Richmond, Virginia. The second was the Board of Domestic Missions, located in Marion, Alabama.

Southern Baptists did not organize a publication or Sunday School Board. Such talk was present in Augusta, however. Some, from the very first, wanted a *Southern* Baptist Publication Board! Other Southern Baptists, pledging loyalty to the ABPS, wanted nothing of the kind. This internal controversy among Southern Baptists dominated Convention life in its first fifty years.

The controversy erupted in Augusta at the organizational meeting of the SBC. William

Sands, editor of *The Religious Herald,* described the Saturday-evening session of that first Southern Baptist Convention meeting:

> We were not present at the commencement of the session, being necessarily absent on the Committee for nominating Boards. When we entered Professor Mell of Mercer University was addressing the Convention with considerable warmth in support of a resolution introduced by J. S. Baker, relative to the expediency of reporting from the Publication Society. In reply to Elder B., the agent of the Publication Society, Elder Burrows, warmly defended the Society. Professor Mell was answered very energetically by Judge Hillyard, who urged the impropriety of immediate separation from societies which had given no just grounds of offense. The resolution was laid on the table; and also one in favor of the Board's engaging in the work of foreign and domestic Bible operations.[3]

At Augusta Southern Baptists were unanimous in the conviction that they must separate from their Northern brethren. They were far from unanimous, however, in the extent of that separation. Some, like Judge Hillyard, held fast to the Publication Society of the North. That point of view won the day in Augusta. And the next year the Convention concluded that it would not "embarrass itself with any enterprise for the publication and sale of books."

Actually that view only half-won. Advocates of the more comprehensive Southern Baptist denominationalism, which included a publication ministry, also half-won. They gathered in Savannah, Georgia, on May 13, 1847, and formed the Southern Baptist Publication Society. Headquartered in Charleston, South Carolina, this society served Southern Baptists from 1847 until 1863. But it never had an official or organic connection with the SBC. Its purpose was "to publish and distribute such books as are needed by the Baptist denomination in the South." Many Southern Baptists switched their allegiance from the ABPS to the SBPS. William B. Johnson, first president of the SBC, was such

a person.[4] Because of the SBPS, the Northern society stayed out of the South from 1847 to the Civil War. By 1863, however, the catastrophe of the war, financial disaster, and Landmarkism helped to bury the Southern Baptist Publication Society. Thread 2 was broken!

Thread 3 was the Bible Board of the Southern Baptist Convention. Unlike the SBPS, the Bible Board was established in 1851 as an integral part of the work of the Convention. Initially, its responsibility was limited to the circulation of the Bible, an assignment given to the Mission Boards by the Convention in 1846. By 1855 the work of the Bible Board had expanded to promote Sunday School work. In the 1850s, therefore, the SBC possessed a Board which exercised the same functions assigned to the later Sunday School Board of 1891. The Bible Board became yet

Basil Manly, Jr.

another casualty of the Civil War. By act of the Convention in 1863, the Bible Board was abolished. A third broken thread!

Like the ancient Egyptian phoenix bird, however, the Southern Baptist commitment to religious education continued to rise from the ashes. In the same meeting of the SBC when the Bible Board was abolished, 1863, Southern Baptists established the Board of Sunday Schools of the Southern Baptist Convention. Here was the fourth thread. By the very hardest, this Board, often called the first Sunday School Board, lasted only ten years. James Frost described the decade of 1863-73 in which the first Board existed as "a decade of almost tragic effort, of noble achievement and of memorable history."[5]

This decade in Southern Baptist history was dominated by two of the "best men God has ever given to the denomination." Both were in their thirties; both were professors at The Southern Baptist Theological Seminary, then located in Greenville, South Carolina; both were sophisticated Southern Baptist scholars who were committed to the Christian education of children; both believed ardently in the value of Sunday Schools; both were crucial in the first Sunday School Board; and both were a part of what Frost called "a royal line" in the Southern Baptist heritage.

Their names? Basil Manly, Jr., and John A. Broadus. Merge the first syllable in Broadus with the first syllable in Manly and you get "Broadman," the present trade name of the general publishing arm of The Sunday School Board of the Southern Baptist Convention. Basil Manly, Jr., secured the recognition of the chair at the 1863 meeting of the SBC in Augusta and offered the following resolution: "*Resolved,* that a committee of seven be appointed to inquire whether it is expedient for this Convention to attempt anything for the promotion of Sunday Schools, and if so what?"[6]

In all truth, however, Manly was not asking an objective question or making a simple inquiry. He wanted a platform to issue the "Manly Manifesto." By being appointed chairman of the committee "to inquire," he got his platform. And the committee report, which he wrote, was his manifesto. Robert A. Baker called it "the first apologetic for the Sunday School movement adopted by the Southern Baptist Convention."[7] It is a beautiful, inspiring, and convincing statement in which Manly said that "the Sunday School is the nursery of the church, the camp of instruction for her young soldiers, the great missionary to the future."[8]

Because Southern Baptists had no general organization engaged in Sunday School work, Manly declared, "Here is at once an open door, and an urgent claim, both opportunity and argument for activity." The SBC followed Manly's leadership and acted by establishing the Board of Sunday Schools of the Southern Baptist Convention. The Convention adopted the following resolution, clearly spelling out what the Board was to do as well as what it was not to do:

John A. Broadus

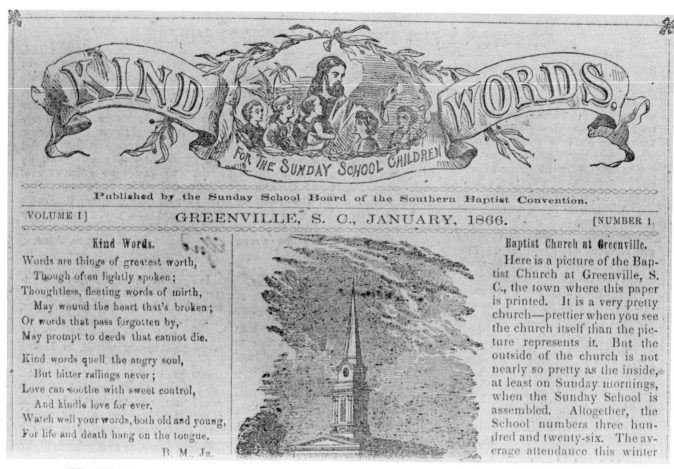

Published by the Sunday School Board of the Southern Baptist Convention.

[VOLUME I]   GREENVILLE, S. C., JANUARY, 1866.   [NUMBER 1.

Kind Words.

Words are things of greatest worth,
 Though often lightly spoken;
Thoughtless, fleeting words of mirth,
 May wound the heart that's broken;
Or words that pass forgotten by,
May prompt to deeds that cannot die.

Kind words quell the angry soul,
 But bitter railings never;
Love can soothe with sweet control,
 And kindle love for ever.
Watch well your words, both old and young,
For life and death hang on the tongue.

B. M., Jr.

Baptist Church at Greenville.

Here is a picture of the Baptist Church at Greenville, S. C., the town where this paper is printed. It is a very pretty church—prettier when you see the church itself than the picture represents it. But the outside of the church is not nearly so pretty as the inside, at least on Sunday mornings, when the Sunday School is assembled. Altogether, the School numbers three hundred and twenty-six. The average attendance this winter

"Kind Words for the Sunday School Children," first published in 1866, was a thread uniting the Board of Sunday Schools of the Southern Baptist Convention (1863-1873) and the Sunday School Board of the Southern Baptist Convention, founded in 1891.

Resolved, that the Board be charged with the duty of taking all measures adopted to promote the establishment, enlargement, and higher efficiency of Sunday Schools throughout our land; provided that the Board shall not establish a printing house.[9]

The closing qualifier was consistent with the 1846 SBC position that the Convention would not "embarrass itself" by launching into the publication business.

This new Board of Sunday Schools was placed in Greenville, South Carolina, home of The Southern Baptist Theological Seminary, Basil Manly, Jr., and John A. Broadus. Manly was elected president of the Board. Broadus became corresponding secretary "with a small salary and with the understanding that he should devote a limited portion of his time to the duties of his office."[10]

The SBC could not meet as scheduled in 1865 because of the Civil War. So when the Convention gathered in 1866 in Russellville, Kentucky, Broadus gave reports for the Board for both years. He carefully listed the titles and descriptions of the Board's publications. These are revealing, reflecting diverse concerns of these early Board leaders.

There were methodology books such as George Taylor's "Hints for Originating and Conducting Sunday Schools" and "A Sunday School Primer" by an anonymous but "distinguished brother in North Carolina." Singing was important, also. With both petite and patriotic titles, two hymn books were "The Little Sunday School Hymn Book" and the "Confederate Sunday School Hymn Book."

Knowing that the Bible was what was most important, the Board published "A Brief Catechism of Bible Doctrine" by J. P. Boyce and "The Child's Question Book on the Four

14

Gospels" and "S.S. Questions on the Four Gospels" by Basil Manly, Jr. This list of titles suggests a couple of facts about this early literature. It was Bible-based and catechetical in character. It was written by some of the best minds Southern Baptists had. Boyce was president and professor of systematic theology at The Southern Baptist Theological Seminary, and Manly taught biblical introduction at the Seminary. Southern Baptist children benefited from Southern Baptist scholars!

One paragraph in Broadus's report of 1866 marked a significant beginning in Southern Baptist publication ministry. That paragraph had to do with the announcement of a small monthly paper entitled *Kind Words for the Sunday School Children*. Broadus wrote of *Kind Words:*

> It was believed that nothing else which it was in our power to do could accomplish so much for the Sunday School Work, as to put forth such a publication. The plan adopted was to issue quite a small sheet, and at a very low price. Children are rather pleased than otherwise that theirs should be a "little" paper, strikingly different from the papers of grown people.[11]

Kind Words became "a golden thread" in Southern Baptist publication history. Published successively in Greenville, South Carolina; Memphis, Tennessee; Marion, Alabama; Macon and Atlanta, Georgia; and finally in Nashville, Tennessee, this little paper for little children continued until 1929. Even then the name was continued to designate a series of leisure-reading periodicals for children until October 1970. J. M. Frost said of the little paper in 1914 that "it is in a great sense the basis of all we have today in Sunday School life and literature."[12]

Now back to Broadus's report to the Southern Baptist Convention in 1866. Throughout most of the document, Broadus was a "corresponding secretary," providing statistics, being accountable, and at points bordering on boredom. But the "preacher" in Broadus could not stay suppressed very long and out came the exhortation: "For the sake of the orphans and all the dear children of the land, for the sake of those coming generations, a regard for whose welfare gives to passing events their chief importance, for the sake of perishing souls, and of Him who died to save, men of Israel, help in this Sunday School work."[13]

Writing to his wife on April 17, 1866, just prior to the Southern Baptist Convention, Broadus said of his work with the Sunday School Board, "I shall lay down that work, positively and altogether." He did lay it down by resigning as corresponding secretary that year. But he never laid it down "altogether." After his resignation and even after this first Sunday School Board closed in 1873, Broadus continued to play a major role in seeing that the new Board of 1891 was established.

After ten years of struggling service to the denomination, the first Sunday School Board was abolished by the Convention in 1873. The reasons were many, some of which shall be suggested later. Suffice it to say that the Board ceased to exist while its work was transferred to the Home Mission Board of the Convention. A fourth broken string!

Actually, this fourth string was not completely broken; it did, however, become woefully weak. A fragile continuity exists between the first Sunday School Board, founded by Manly and Broadus, and the new Sunday School Board founded by J. M. Frost in 1891. That fragile continuity is the Home Mission Board of the SBC. And it was fragile! The Home Mission Board suffered seriously from complications following the Civil War.

After 1873 the complications were compounded by the added responsibility of having to shoulder the work of the defunct Sunday School Board. The Home Mission Board grew weaker and weaker. By 1880 a resolution before the SBC in Lexington, Kentucky, requested an inquiry and report "upon, the expediency of consolidating the work of the Home and Foreign Boards, and of appointing but one Board upon missionary work."[14] A special committee recommended against consolidation, and the Home Mission Board survived. The Board, however, could give little attention to the promotion of Sunday Schools.

Samuel Boykin

Two men made a difference during these difficult years. They were I. T. Tichenor and Samuel Boykin. Tichenor became corresponding secretary of the Home Mission Board in 1882. Former pastor of First Church, Montgomery, Alabama, and First Church, Memphis, Tennessee, Tichenor had also been the first president of Auburn University, where he served from 1872 until 1882. He left Auburn to accept the unenviable position of leader of a tottering denominational agency.

Tichenor went to work. He moved the Home Mission Board from Marion, Alabama, to Atlanta, Georgia. He traveled. He preached. He wrote. He used every gift God had given him to call Southern Baptists to their potential in poverty-stricken days. Southern Baptists responded and rallied! And they did because Tichenor instilled a denominational consciousness in them.

He made them proud of being *Southern* Baptists. Tichenor believed, however, that a central key to denominationalizing Southern Baptists was a Southern Baptist agency charged to produce religious literature and promote Sunday School. Southern Baptists had to have a Sunday School Board of some kind! Frost said of Tichenor, "No one surpassed the new Secretary as dreamer of dreams and seer of visions in denominational needs and power of conquest, and not many equaled him in making others through his eloquence on the platform see what he saw and believe what he believed."[15]

Tichenor certainly caused Frost to see what he saw and believe what he believed. Frost himself would literally dream a dream that issued in the Sunday School Board of 1891. Consciously or unconsciously, Frost was obviously under Tichenor's spell. Frost recalled, in the first history of the Sunday School Board, a midnight conversation he had with Tichenor in Selma, Alabama:

> Though after midnight we stood at the gate of his friend, Captain Hugh Haralson, with whom he was stopping, and talked for two hours. Rather he talked and I listened. I was sympathetic, but unable to follow his sweep of thought in outlining the future, showing what the Baptists of the South might accomplish, and the imperative need that a people make their own literature.[16]

As corresponding secretary of the Home Mission Board, Tichenor reviewed Southern Baptist interests in making their own literature. Tichenor's work in the 1880s made the Sunday School Board a possibility in the early 1890s.

Samuel Boykin, unlike Tichenor, was not the charismatic type. Partially deaf, he did not rally the forces; but he did stay at his desk, editing *Kind Words,* a children's paper, for thirty years. Working as editor of *Kind Words* for the first Sunday School Board, he continued his work in that capacity when *Kind Words* shifted to the Home Mission Board. In 1892 he became the second member, after James Frost, of the 1891 Sunday School Board staff.

In 1916 the Sunday School Board made a $10,000 gift to the Home Mission Board, half of which was to be the Samuel Boykin Memorial Fund in memory of Boykin as "the chief pioneer and genius in making Sunday School literature for the Baptists of the South."[17]

Why, with the likes of Manly, Broadus, Tichenor, and Boykin, were there so many "broken threads" from 1845 to 1891? Why couldn't Southern Baptists sustain efforts at building a general agency to coordinate and promote Sunday School work and publications? Several reasons have already been given. First, the Civil War and the era of Reconstruction hurt Southern Baptist institutional life badly. The Southern Baptist Theological Seminary of Greenville, South Carolina, for example, almost folded. So did the Home Mission Board. Both had to move to find a base for beginning again. Southern Seminary settled in Louisville, Kentucky, in 1877; the Home Mission Board found refuge in Atlanta in 1882. Efforts at establishing and sustaining a Sunday School agency died *during* the war and *after* the war. It was difficult to launch or to last!

Second, questions emerged regarding the constitutionality of the SBC having a general Board for such purposes. "Did the SBC Constitution allow such?" some would ask. And Basil Manly, Jr., countered in 1863 "that the subject comes fairly within the range of the Constitution, and accords with the design of this Convention is unquestionable."[18] Some felt, however, that the SBC Constitution allowed only for the Home and Foreign Mission Boards. Moreover, they thought these were sufficient for all the purposes of the Convention.

Three, early efforts on behalf of publications and Sunday School promotion were often related to The Southern Baptist Theological Seminary. An existing prejudice toward the seminary tainted the Sunday School and publication efforts. A. E. Dickinson wrote Basil Manly, Jr., soon after the formation of the first Sunday School Board and said, "It will not do for the Greenville professors to do all the book-making. That has already been anticipated by a few grumblers that I know of."[19]

Four, state conventions had been involved in Sunday School work prior to the organization of the SBC in 1845. Some wanted to let each individual state convention champion the cause. Manly and others wanted centralization for better efficiency. Thomas E. Skinner of North Carolina wrote John A. Broadus, "Tell

Brother Manly to push on with the Sunday school work. I am a 'centralization Baptist.' "[20]

Five, some Southern Baptists preferred interdenominational societies, such as the American Sunday School Union, to lead out in this work. Six, strong sentiment prevailed to continue working with the American Baptist Publication Society of the North. Representing a continuity of heritage between Baptists North and South, this was one of the most emotion-laden and persuasive arguments against Southern Baptist action.

Seven, private publishers, J. R. Graves in particular, wanted to provide religious publications and thereby promote Sunday School work. Graves, the father of Landmarkism, towered above much of Southern Baptist life in the nineteenth century. Landmarkism, claiming Baptist churches to be the only true churches and, therefore, having unbroken historical continuity with New Testament churches, wanted desperately to control publication efforts.

Graves was basically an independent who did not want cooperation through denominational Boards unless he controlled them. Baker correctly wrote of Graves, "He played an influential role in every Southern Baptist effort before 1981 to provide literature and leadership for the Sunday School movement."[21] Graves created the Southern Baptist Sunday School Union in 1857 as competition for the Southern Baptist Publication Society and gained control of the Bible Board of the SBC and the first Sunday School Board. Denominational politicking, theological differences, monetary greed, and human arrogance helped break several threads.

Other factors militated against success, also: economic depression, such as in 1873; financial mismanagement; and the obvious psychological fact that failure breeds fear of failure. Southern Baptists almost became experts at failing in this venture.

Then how, in the face of repeated failures, did Southern Baptists keep coming back to try again? What ultimately caused the success of 1891? More will have to be said of this later, but four factors deserve highlighting at this point. One was the desire for specific denominational identity. A process of denominationalizing occurred among Southern Baptists in the nineteenth century. Some, like Tichenor, believed that for Baptists of the South to become denominationalized, they must produce *their* literature and promote *their* Sunday Schools.

Practically, this meant two things. Southern Baptists should support their own rather than interdenominational efforts such as the American Sunday School Union. Manly was speaking specifically of that Union when he wrote, "While all the valuable service formerly rendered by that organization is cheerfully acknowledged, your Committee believes that the time has come for us, *as a denomination*, to commence this work on our own account, with no unfriendliness or ungenerous feeling toward others."[22]

The spirit of denominationalism also meant growing separation from Baptists of the North in regard to publication and Sunday School concerns. The desire for clear denominational identity was a major catalyst for the repeated efforts of Southern Baptists to form a Sunday School Board. Moreover—and here is a subtheme of this book—after its organization in 1891, no institution has done more to denominationalize Southern Baptists than has this Board.

A second factor motivating Southern Baptists to organize their own Board, and also fueling denominationalism, was the powerful post-Civil War feeling of regionalism. Prior to 1845 Baptists in the South perceived themselves as just that—Baptists *in* the South. After the rupture of 1845 Baptists *in* the South began perceiving themselves as *Southern* Baptists. With the fading of a national Baptist spirit, regionalism intensified denominationalism.

Three, Southern Baptists kept trying to knit the threads back together because of a commitment to evangelism and a belief that the Sunday School movement was a major strategy for evangelism and Bible study. Four, they kept coming back because of "a royal line." Leadership, then as now, was the key. Manly, Broadus, Tichenor, Boykin, and others formed "a royal line." Fortunately, it did not end with them.

Notes

1. J. M. Frost, *The Sunday School Board, Southern Baptist Convention: Its History and Work* (Nashville: Sunday School Board, N. O.), p. 12.

2. Southern Baptist Convention *Annual*, 1892, p. lvi.

3. *The Religious Herald*, May 22, 1845, vol. 3, no. 15.

4. *The Religious Herald*, May 21, 1846.

5. Frost, *The Sunday School Board*, p. 8.

6. Southern Baptist Convention *Annual*, 1863, p. 12.

7. Robert A. Baker, *The Story of the Sunday School Board* (Nashville: Convention Press, 1966), p. 14.

8. Southern Baptist Convention *Annual*, 1863, p. 45.

9. Ibid., p. 47.

10. Southern Baptist Convention *Annual*, 1866, p. 24.

11. Southern Baptist Convention *Annual*, 1866, p. 30.

12. Frost, *The Sunday School Board*, p. 9.

13. Southern Baptist Convention *Annual*, 1866, p. 28.

14. Southern Baptist Convention *Annual*, 1880, p. 15.

15. Frost, *The Sunday School Board*, pp. 9-10.

16. Ibid., p. 11.

17. *Encyclopedia of Southern Baptists*, vol. 1, p. 185.

18. Southern Baptist Convention *Annual*, 1863, p. 45.

19. Basil Manly Correspondence, Dargan-Carver Library, "Folder 6."

20. Ibid.

21. Baker, *The Story of the Sunday School Board*, p. 9.

22. Southern Baptist Convention *Annual*, 1863, p. 46.

At the 1891 Southern Baptist Convention in Birmingham, Alabama, the report which recommended the creation of a Sunday School publishing board was formulated through compromise by J. B. Gambrell and J. M. Frost (upper right). Because the O'Brien Opera House was crowded to overflowing, Frost had to be lifted through a window (left) to present his report. An emotional appeal for peace by John A. Broadus (lower right) broke the tension, and the report was adopted.

20

2 Frost, Bell, and "a Dream Defended"

B. W. Spilman, a three-hundred-pounder, became the first field secretary of the Southern Baptist Sunday School Board in 1901. He worked in that capacity until his retirement in 1940. Appropriately, his co-workers nicknamed him "the Sunday School Man." Before joining the Sunday School Board, he was Sunday School secretary for the North Carolina Baptist State Convention. While tramping all over the state trying to stir up interest in Sunday School work, he received a long, friendly, discouraging letter from John E. White, corresponding secretary of the state convention. In short, White said that the people of North Carolina would not support Sunday School work, that nothing but failure awaited Spilman's efforts, and that he would help Spilman secure a pastorate if the round man wished.

Spilman put the letter in his pocket and set out for his next engagement. A few days later he was back in his office in Raleigh. Pulling out the letter, he read it again. Then he reached for the small dictionary on his desk, turned the pages to "failure," and with careful deliberation drew a line through it!

That is what the earliest leaders of the Sunday School Board did—they drew a line through failure. Two of those leaders were J. M. Frost and T. P. Bell. Frost was the founder and first executive of the Board; Bell, his close friend, was the second executive. Frost had a dream; Bell defended it.

With the death of the first Sunday School Board in 1873, Sunday School functions were transferred to the Home Mission Board. As indicated earlier, however, the Home Mission Board experienced serious reversals in the 1870s. Tichenor became the leader of that Board in 1882. And by 1885 the Home Mission Board began a comeback. That resurgence brought a revitalization of the Sunday School functions of the Board. But with that revitalization also came renewed conflict.

The issue was clear-cut. Should the Southern Baptist Convention provide Sunday School literature for Baptist churches of the South or leave that to the American Baptist Publication Society of Philadelphia? "Shall we attempt it," asked Tichenor, "or shall we surrender it to others?"[1] Tichenor led the Home Mission Board and Southern Baptists to attempt it! In 1886 he announced to the Convention that the Home Mission Board would begin publishing "a full grade of *Quarterlies* three in number, and a *Magazine for Teachers*."[2]

Opposition was prompt, vigorous, and vitriolic. J. M. Frost witnessed the turbulent Southern Baptist Convention meetings of 1887 in Louisville, 1888 in Richmond, and 1889 in Memphis, "the severest of them all." It became, at times, he said, "almost a war on the Home Mission Board" and Tichenor.[3] In the face of repeated past failures, some Southern Baptists just did not want to try again. Most of the opposition, however, came from friends of the ABPS. And the ABPS itself, "through its friends, and by all the forces at its command, withstood the Home Board movement" and "even claimed to have preempted the field and challenged the right

James Marion Frost

of the Convention to publish Sunday school materials."[4]

The SBC appointed a committee at Richmond in 1888 to confer with three Northern Baptist agencies "to adjust all questions of difference which may have arisen." After reporting on progress made with two of the agencies, the committee told the 1889 meeting of the SBC, "We also had a conference, full and free, with the representatives of the American Baptist Publication Society, and we were unable to arrive at any agreement."[5] That disagreement, degenerating at times into bitter struggle, lasted until the ABPS withdrew its branch houses from the South in 1910.

In a classic understatement, Frost said the controversy "was somewhat enlarged" in 1890. Frost himself did the enlarging! He "made the issue more sharp and concrete."

Although a longtime friend and supporter of the ABPS, Frost made the audacious proposal that Southern Baptists establish a new Sunday School Board. Why? Had he not been able to forget that midnight conversation with I. T. Tichenor in Selma, Alabama? Or had Tichenor "hooked" him by asking him to write for the new graded series in 1887? Or did he simply feel that he was acting under command of a dream from God? His description refuses to let the historian play with paraphrase. Here are his words:

> Since the Convention at Memphis the preceding year I had gone from Selma to Richmond as pastor of the Leigh Street Baptist Church, and was living in the parsonage on Libby Hill, at No. 5 Twenty-ninth Street. One night the latter part of January I awakened from sleep with the thought of a New Board in full possession, and stirring my soul in such way as I make no effort here to describe, and for which I make no unusual claim. It worked itself out in a set of resolutions which I determined while lying there to present to the Fort Worth Convention. They were written out in the early morning light, and were shown first that very morning, when *en route* to my study to Dr. T. P. Bell, now of the *Christian Index,* but then with the Foreign Mission Board, and a member of the Leigh Street Church. He at once gave his earnest approval, and said the resolutions would be "a clarion call to the Baptists of the South."[6]

Frost gave yet a crisper summary of the idea for the Sunday School Board, "I crave the privilege of saying in the simplest way, God touched me and I thought it."[7]

On February 27, 1890, *The Religious Herald* published six resolutions by Frost, which he said would be submitted to the Southern Baptist Convention in Fort Worth, Texas, in May 1890. In the intervening weeks Baptist papers debated the proposals. Only two of the papers, Frost recalled later, supported him. They were the *Baptist and Reflector* of Tennessee and the *Western Recorder* of Kentucky.

22

J. B. Gambrell

Keeping his promise, Frost presented his resolutions in Fort Worth. But there he ran into J. B. Gambrell, destined to become one of Southern Baptists' most influential leaders and at that time editor of *The Baptist Record* of Mississippi. Gambrell strongly resisted separation from the ABPS. Instead of the Board of Publications which he wanted, Frost had to settle for a Sunday School Committee. The decision was a compromise, so it kept the controversy alive for another year. Would it be settled in Birmingham in 1891?

In its report to the SBC in Birmingham, the Sunday School Committee concluded by requesting "a considerable enlargement of the powers of the committee, or what is much better, the appointment of a Board to whom these great interests can be entrusted."[8] Frost jumped to his feet and moved that a special committee be appointed to consider the request. Frost chaired the special committee composed of one man from each state. J. B. Gambrell represented Mississippi. This committee knew where the "rub" was, so its members asked Frost and Gambrell to meet and draw up the report to be submitted to the Convention!

The two men met in an "upper room" in the old Florence Hotel. Frost described it this way: "After much conferring together, and at the close of a conference which lasted practically all day, he proposed to let me write the report and even name the location of the Board, provided he could write the closing paragraph."[9] Frost consented, provided Gambrell would let Frost write the last sentence.

Here is Gambrell's "closing paragraph."

In conclusion your committee, in its long and earnest consideration of this whole matter in all its environments, have been compelled to take account of the well known fact, that there are widely divergent views held among us by brethren equally earnest, consecrated and devoted to the best interest of the Master's Kingdom. It is therefore, recommended that the fullest freedom of choice be accorded to every one as to what literature he will use or support, and that no brother be disparaged in the slightest degree on account of what he may do in the exercise of his right as Christ's freeman.

Here is Frost's closing sentence: "But we would earnestly urge all brethren to give to this Board a fair consideration, and in no case to obstruct it in the great work assigned it by this Convention."[10]

The full committee accepted the Frost-Gambrell document. When it came time for

O'Brien Opera House, Birmingham, Alabama: scene of 1891 Southern Baptist Convention

the report to be submitted to the Convention, the house was packed. In fact, Frost, who was to give the report, had to be lifted through a window to get into the building. Everyone expected a hot debate. As soon as Frost finished giving the report to the Convention and before even he could speak to it, John A. Broadus, then president of Southern Seminary and the most influential Southern Baptist alive, was on the platform. He made a brief speech about not making speeches. Not another word was spoken except cries of "Question!" "Question!" The report was adopted overwhelmingly. Broadus had "put a lid on the volcano." In the words of W. H. Whitsitt, some of the brethren had "screwed their courage to the sticking place"; and the Southern Baptist Convention had a Sunday School Board! The "royal line" had reasserted itself.

Immediately following the adoption of the report, J. B. Gambrell presented a paper signed by him and Joshua Levering, nominating Frost as corresponding secretary for the new Board. Frost remembered the experience:

> It not only surprised but fairly startled me. I begged that it should not come to a vote, and protested that I could not consider it for a moment. They were kindly, acceded to my earnest plea, and the Convention instructed the New Board to elect its own secretary.[11]

The Board met Tuesday, May 26, in the study of Dr. W. R. L. Smith, pastor of the First Baptist Church in Nashville and recently named chairman of the new Sunday School Board. A major item of business was at hand—the election of a corresponding secretary. Two men were nominated, J. M. Frost of Richmond, Virginia, and Lansing Burrows, pastor of First Church, Augusta, Georgia. The vote ended in a tie. Remembering Frost's sincere appeal at the Convention, the man who nominated him, E. E. Folk, switched his vote; and Burrows was elected. Dr. Burrows, however, declined the position.

Meeting again on June 12, the Board unanimously elected, in spite of his earlier protests, J. M. Frost as corresponding secretary. The

call of the Board threw him "into consternation." Then he received a letter from Dr. John A. Broadus which made him feel that he should "at least stop and listen to the brethren." While struggling with the decision to leave the pastorate which he "loved with a passion well-nigh consuming," he visited with Henry G. Weston, president of Crozer Seminary, in Philadelphia. On Sunday evening he attended the Fifth Baptist Church to hear Dr. Ezekiel Robinson preach. In that sermon, Frost said, "He told in a touching, telling way how sometimes God crosses all our plans, turns our purposes aside, and constrains us into new lines of life. The message went home to my heart as a message from God—a voice that would not be hushed."[12] He returned to Richmond and offered his resignation as pastor of the Leigh Street Baptist Church.

In his agreement with Gambrell in the Florence Hotel, Frost named the location of the Board. He chose Nashville, though "there were strong undercurrents" for Louisville, Kentucky. Louisville had been the one-year home of the Sunday School Committee, established at the Convention in 1890. Moreover, Louisville, since 1877, had been the home of Southern Seminary, John A. Broadus, and Basil Manly, Jr. But Nashville constituted a good choice because it was the chief printing center of the South and the geographical center of the Convention territory.

Frost assumed his new task on July 1, 1891. "The first Sunday in Nashville," he said, "was the most lonesome day of my life." With money borrowed from a family inheritance of his wife,[13] he left Richmond with only the desk on which he wrote the original resolutions calling for the establishment of the Board. At the gracious invitation of E. E. Folk, editor of the *Baptist and Reflector,* Frost placed his desk, rent-free, in Folk's office. And that was the beginning of the Sunday School Board of the Southern Baptist Convention! Ninety years later the Board employs approximately fifteen hundred people, operates an annual budget of 109 million dollars, and owns property in the book value amount of 33 million dollars. Broadus used to

The Founders' Room, located off the main lobby of the Board, is a replica of the 1884 pastor's study of the First Baptist Church, Nashville, Tennessee, where, in 1891, J. M. Frost was elected corresponding secretary of the newly formed Sunday School Board.

Frost and his secretary, Ethel Allen, work in his office.

have a saying: "Watch the beginning of things!"

On January 1, 1892, Samuel Boykin joined Frost as editor-in-chief. In that capacity Boykin continued to edit *Kind Words* and other publications. Boykin died on November 3, 1899, after forty years of leadership among Southern Baptists in connection with Sunday School literature. Thirty of those years he had been the editor of *Kind Words*.

After serving only eighteen months as the chief executive of the infant Board, J. M. Frost resigned to become pastor of the First Baptist Church of Nashville. In those few months, however, he had given staying power to the Board. Personalizing the Board, Frost traveled throughout the Convention territory, "campaigning the state conventions." He wanted to win over the reluctant and make visible the ministry of the Board. Circulation of the Board's publications, inherited from the Home Mission Board and Sunday School Committee, increased. The financial vitality of the Board was proven. At the end of the first fiscal year, the Board had paid all of its bills and had a balance "of over one thousand ($1,000) dollars!" "This was a surprise to us all," said Frost, "and threw a new light on the future."[14]

Frost left the Board to return to his love—the pastorate. He had served from 1891 until 1893; he would return to the Board again in 1896 and serve it until his death in 1916. In his first Board report to the Southern Baptist Convention in 1892, Frost ecstatically wrote that "instead of the Board's being distractive and a stirrer-up of strife, it now promises to be a unifying element in our denominational life." The dream had become reality! And Frost was right; the Board did become "a unifying element" and a denominationalizer.

Frost overspoke in that report, however, when he maintained, "All opposition and strife and discord are gone—or seem going." The dream still had to be defended! And the man largely responsible for that is one of the most unknown, underrated, and unafraid figures in the Board's history. Though always a gentleman, he had a fighting spirit and was fearless in stating his convictions.[15] Serving the briefest period, only three years (from 1893

until 1896), of all the Board's leaders, he must be numbered among the ablest. His name was Theodore Percy Bell.

Preeminently, Bell should be remembered as "Defender of the Dream." He had been the first person to see the dream on paper. On the morning after his dream, Frost showed his proposed resolutions to T. P. Bell. Later, Frost recalled Bell's reaction:

> He at once gave his earnest approval, and said the resolutions would be "a clarion call to the Baptists of the South." He knew more of the affair in its relation to me as the time went on than any other person, was always earnest in support, a constant guide, inspiration and joy as the conflict thickened.[15]

At that time, 1890, Frost was pastor of Leigh Street Church in Richmond, and Bell was assistant corresponding secretary of the Foreign Mission Board and a member of Frost's church. Bell had been with the Foreign Mission Board three and one-half years.

Born in Beaufort, South Carolina, in 1852, Bell experienced, as a boy, the bitterness of the Civil War. He graduated from The Southern Baptist Theological Seminary in 1880, "in the opinion of his instructors and fellow-students, one of the most promising that had ever gone forth from that school."[16] Following graduation, he served for six years as pastor of First Baptist Church, Anderson, South Carolina.

Bell's highest commitment, lasting throughout his life, was to foreign missions. After seminary, he had been a missions volunteer, only to be rejected because he did not accept the "dictation theory" of biblical inspiration.[17] Though rejecting him as a missionary, the Foreign Mission Board hired him as assistant secretary and made him editor of the *Foreign Mission Journal*. After one month at the Sunday School Board, he was elected corresponding secretary of the Foreign Mission Board, but declined to accept.

Out of his background, Bell brought several characteristics to the Sunday School Board in 1893. He brought his red-blooded "southernness," one of his most salient characteristics. He brought a commitment to denominational-

Theodore Percy Bell

ism and a vision of the Sunday School Board as an instrument of missions. He also brought visibility. Because of his extensive travels and speaking on behalf of the Foreign Mission Board, he was much better known throughout the Convention than Frost had been in 1891. Moreover, he brought the experience of working for a denominational agency. As important as all the rest, however, he brought plainspokenness, aggressiveness, and a willingness to defend the Sunday School Board.

Bell defended the Board, by careful management, in the face of a potential financial crisis. By the time Bell came to the Board, the nation was feeling the impact of the financial panic of 1892. In his first full year, Bell helped to increase receipts at the Board by $5,500. In 1895 the Board set aside its first reserve fund—only $1,000, but quite an accomplishment in a year of "almost unprecedented business depression."[18]

Bell beefed up the defense of the Board by bringing in new recruits. In January 1894 he conscripted thirty-three-year-old Isaac J. Van Ness, pastor of Immanuel Baptist Church in Nashville, to edit *Young People's Leader,* the Board's first publication for the Baptist Young People's Union. Van Ness would eventually serve for thirty-five years in a full-time capacity with the Board. Eighteen of those years he would spend as the third corresponding secretary.

Bell also defended the Board in its continuing struggle with the American Baptist Publication Society. He believed, and with justification, that the Society wanted a monopoly on all Baptist publishing in the country. In fact, Bell said, the Society was just as determined to destroy the Board as Grant was to destroy Lee. One great defeat by the North was enough for this man from Dixie! In a letter to a friend Bell queried himself, "I wonder sometimes if I belong to an old school that is too strongly *Southern* Baptist in its sentiment."

A good strategist, Bell knew that the best defense is a good offense. So he took to the road. He attended numerous Southern Baptist meetings, promoting the Board and its materials by his effective preaching. "I expect to be a gatling gun doing no little execution in

our behalf,"[19] he once wrote. He labored solely for Baptist interests of the South.

One area of the Board's work which Bell accentuated was its missionary task. He believed that the Board's literature could be made the most powerful missionary agency possible in teaching and developing children in the Sunday Schools. When he pushed the periodicals, he felt he was working for home and foreign missions. And that was what he had always wanted to do.

In March 1896, Bell resigned from the Board to become editor of the *Christian Index,* the state Baptist paper of Georgia. He believed that the work of the Board had prospered and stabilized so that his resignation would not hurt the Board's effectiveness. Frost said that Bell had "set the new enterprise forward in a masterful way." Historians have been correct in giving Frost a more prominent place than Bell in the early days of the Board. But Frost himself needs to be heard in assessing Bell's role. In a personal letter which Frost wrote Bell near the end of both of their lives, Frost said: "Few men if any have come into my life with more power than you and it was always for good, both for me personally and for my relation to others. The public will never know how much is due you for any and everything that I have done."[20]

Bell reaped the benefits of Frost's dream, but Frost reaped the benefits of Bell's defense of the dream. In 1896 Frost resigned his Nashville pastorate to assume, for the second time, the leadership of the Board. He vowed to God and his brethren that he would stay as long as he was needed. He stayed until his death in 1916.

Upon returning to the Board, Frost immediately encountered the opposition of the American Baptist Publication Society. Prompted by its Southern friends and in the name of harmony and unity, the Society made unbelievable proposals which amounted to the absorption of the Board by the Society. The proposals, which came from Dr. A. J. Rowland of the Society, were presented to the members of the Sunday School Board by Frost. The Board was unanimous in its response: "We have no thought whatever of surrendering the work entrusted to us by the

28

Southern Baptist Convention."[21]

Rebuffed, the Society decided to go public with their offer. Hoping both to embarrass the Board and to solicit support at the 1896 meeting of the SBC in Chattanooga, the Society appealed publicly to Baptists of the South to support the Society proposal. Nothing came of this seething volcano in 1896. But when the Convention met in 1897 in Wilmington, North Carolina, the eruption occurred. One representative of the Society made an open attack on the Board, challenging its corresponding secretary. It created intense resentment. A number wanted to respond in kind. Frost said, "I never saw so many heavy guns unlimber so quickly and get ready for action."[22]

William E. Hatcher, prominent pastor of Grace Street Church in Richmond, claimed the floor. He used all the gifts in his oratorical storehouse—humor, pungent statement, and pathos. "He came to the close like thunder in the gathering storm" and said, "I have been a life-long friend of the Publication Society, but it must not come here to interfere with our work. We have our way of doing things, and woe betide the man who crosses our path."[23]

Hatcher's speech helped deliver the death blow to the work of the Society in the South. His speech certainly articulated the growing denominational consciousness of the SBC. That consciousness had helped to create the Board. Now the Board was intensifying that consciousness. Other skirmishes occurred between the Board and the Society, but by 1910 the long war of competition had ended. The South had won! The ABPS withdrew all of its branch houses from the South in 1910.

To be sure, much of the early life of the Sunday School Board under Frost and Bell, a period from 1891 until 1916, was a struggle for survival. But that is by no means the whole story. Ministry to the churches was more important to Frost and Bell than was institutional survival. Multiple forms of ministry were reaching out from the Board by the end of Frost's era. Multiple ministries demanded more ministers. New names and new programs appeared on Sunday School Board stationery and curriculum materials. A history was evolving.

B. W. Spilman

New programs as well as new faces appeared to help denominationalize some interdenominational movements. One such program was Sunday School Teacher Training. The face that went with it was Bernard Washington Spilman, one of the cherished and noble names in Southern Baptist Sunday School history. He joined the Board as its first field secretary in May 1901, after serving in Sunday School work in North Carolina. His office was the "field," and his study was in railroad trains.

At the turn of the century, certain interdenominational efforts were being made on behalf of teacher training; but few, if any, denominations had undertaken such ministry.

In addition to his Sunday School work, B. W. Spilman, who weighed 300 pounds, was well known as a humorist.

Spilman helped "Southern Baptistize" teacher training. Frost claimed that Spilman was the first person to put teacher training on the map in the South. The Board published Spilman's tiny book *Normal Studies for Sunday School Workers* one year after he came to the Board. Others joined Spilman in his work at the Board. Many of them, like Spilman,

had long, productive tenures which helped shape the tradition of the Board. Some of those and their years of service were Spilman, 1901-1940; Landrum Pinson Leavell, 1903-29; Harvey Beauchamp, 1905-38; Ernest Eugene Lee, 1909-46; Arthur Flake, 1909-36; Annie Laurie Williams, 1909-32; P. E. Burroughs, 1910-43; and Margaret A. Frost, 1910-41.

A second interdenominational movement which the Board brought under denominational control was the Baraca-Philathea Movement. This movement, which began in 1890 in Syracuse, New York, consisted of Adult Bible classes which sustained only loose relationship to the churches. Loyalties were often more class-oriented than church-directed.

In its 1912 report to the SBC, the Board acknowledged that organizing adult Bible classes was one of the latest trends of the Sunday School movement. The Board encouraged the movement, made practical suggestions regarding names for the classes, and stressed that the classes should be listed with the Board as the Convention Adult Bible Class Department. This would aid in marking the classes as Baptist and identifying them with "all the great interests fostered by the Convention."[24] Eventually these classes accepted denominational leadership. The movement significantly increased the number of adults in Bible study, and the Baraca-Philathea Movement had also been "Southern Baptistized." P. E. Burroughs and Harry L. Strickland spearheaded this denominationalizing process at the Board.

The Board assimilated a youth movement for the denomination, also. The Christian Endeavor Movement, an interdenominational youth movement, developed in this country in the 1880s. American denominations, fearful of losing their youth, began forming denominational societies. By 1891 the Baptist Young People's Union of America was organized. Within three years the Board was publishing BYPU literature (*Young People's Leader*, 1894). And the Convention, at the prompting of the Board, was adopting a resolution recommending that young people's unions "be strictly denominational." By 1918 full responsibility for BYPU was entrusted to the Board.

While this process of denominationalizing nondenominational movements was not unique to Southern Baptists, no denomination was more effective with the process than the SBC. Without the Sunday School Board, one wonders if the Convention would have accomplished the process. And without J. M. Frost one wonders how effective the Board would have been. He was a committed denominationalist. In fact, I. J. Van Ness said that Frost had a touch of the Landmarker in him. Frost thought, said Van Ness, that the Baptists were "it."[25]

The early history of the Board, however, was not one of Landmark sectarianism, isolationism, and independence. Frost had some similarities with Graves, but he had some major differences. Frost was more committed to denominational cooperation than a true Landmarker would allow. In denominational matters, like Basil Manly, Jr., and the "royal line," Frost was very much a "Board" Baptist. But he was *Baptist!*

So in the twenty-five-year Frost-Bell era, the Board strengthened the denomination by taming movements which could have eroded denominationalism. But the Board took other actions which helped to draw more tightly the cords on the denominational garment. For one thing, the Board helped to create a "Convention spirit" among the agencies by its contribution to and support of those agencies. By 1916 the Board had committed support, monetary or otherwise, to all the state conventions as well as to the Foreign Mission Board, the Home Mission Board, the Woman's Mis-

sionary Union, the Layman's Missionary Movement, the Education Committee, and The Southern Baptist Theological Seminary.

The Board had also published a hymnal in 1904 which initiated the process of standardizing worship in Southern Baptist churches. Ridgecrest, a national Southern Baptist assembly, was endorsed and later operated by the Board. A Southern Baptist student ministry had begun in 1915, eventually to become the responsibility of the Board. The Board established a Home Department in 1898, and groundwork was gradually laid for a Church Architecture department. Because of the expanding ministries of the Board, Southern Baptist churches did not need to look beyond their own denomination for guidance.

A major development in the life of the Board occurred in 1898. That was the year it published its first book. And that was without authorization from the Convention! When the Board was organized at the 1891 Convention in Birmingham, a strong prejudice existed against the Board ever engaging in publication of books. Robert Baker gave three reasons for this attitude. One, some Southern Baptists, in the tradition of J. R. Graves, simply felt that a denomination should not engage in the book-publishing business. Two, some saw it as another unnecessary area of competition with the ABPS. Three, some objected to the financial risks involved.

In 1891, therefore, the Convention constructed the "Birmingham Barrier" to any publication other than that connected with Sunday School work.[26] J. M. Frost broke that

31

The Sunday School Board was housed for a time at the Methodist Publishing House. Frost said the Methodists "furnished rooms without expense and with every convenience and courtesy."

The Board's first home of its own was a residence at 167 Fourth Avenue, North.

barrier when he secured Board approval in December 1897 to publish *The Story of Yates the Missionary* by President Charles E. Taylor of Wake Forest College. In its next annual session, the Convention commended the Board and, in effect, removed the barrier.

The Board was certainly a new but extensive and influential presence in the Southern Baptist Convention by the time of Frost's death. For several years, however, its physical appearance would not have suggested such. Frost, you remember, began with borrowed funds and his own desk in a corner of the office of the Tennessee Baptist state paper. The "office" was compliments of Editor Folk of the *Baptist and Reflector*. After six

months the Board moved to the Presbyterian Publishing House for a short while. The Methodist Publishing House was the Board's next home. Frost said that the Methodists "furnished rooms without expense and with every convenience and courtesy" and they "almost carried the Sunday School Board in those early days."

The Board's first home of its own was a residence at 167 Fourth Avenue, North. From there the Board moved to a residence at 710 Church Street. In October 1913, twenty-two years after its founding, the Board moved into its new building at 161 Eighth Avenue, North. This building, redecorated and rededicated in 1980, is a monument to J. M. Frost.

Above: From Fourth Avenue, the Board moved to 710 Church Street.
Opposite page: In 1913 the Board occupied its new headquarters at 161 Eighth Avenue, North, which today is known as the Frost Building.

Dr. W. R. L. Smith, pastor of the First Baptist Church in Nashville, was the first president (chairman) of the Board. When Frost assumed the position of corresponding secretary in 1891, Smith said to him, "Be patient—I give you twenty-five years in which to make good with your task." Smith was correct. By 1900 80 percent of all Baptist Sunday Schools in the South secured their literature from the Board. In 1892 the Board had total receipts of only $19,574.83. On the twentieth anniversary of the Board in 1911, receipts were $278,446.69! Five years later, when Frost gave his last report to the Convention, the receipts had skyrocketed to $452,729.24! In its first twenty-five years the

Board had literally paid denominational dividends. Under Frost and Bell the Board gave $786,088.26 to other SBC agencies and interests.

In those twenty-five years the Board had placed the Bible at the center of the church's study. It had promoted and popularized the Sunday School as the means of nurturing and evangelizing. It had undergirded and strengthened a missions emphasis which had characterized Southern Baptists since 1845. It had helped to create and intensify a Southern Baptist denominational identity.

It began with one man's dream. The task was one of making brick without straw. But James Marion Frost, Theodore Percy Bell, and their associates were part of "a royal line." They knew how to ink through "failure."

Notes

1. SBC *Annual*, 1885, p. vii.
2. SBC *Annual*, 1886, p. xii.
3. Frost, *The Sunday School Board*, p. 11.
4. Ibid.
5. SBC *Annual*, 1889, p. 11.
6. Frost, *The Sunday School Board*, pp. 14-15.
7. Ibid., p. 14.
8. SBC *Annual*, 1891, p. 11.
9. Frost, *The Sunday School Board*, p. 19.
10. SBC *Annual*, 1891, p. 23.
11. Frost, *The Sunday School Board*, p. 21.
12. Ibid., p. 91.
13. Joe W. Burton, *Road to Nashville* (Nashville: Broadman Press, 1977), p. 107.
14. Frost, *The Sunday School Board*, p. 36.
15. Ibid., p. 15.
16. Norman W. Cox, "Theodore Percy Bell" (Founder's Day Address, Sunday School Board, May 10, 1957), p. 2.
17. Ibid.
18. See Robert A. Baker, *The Story of the Sunday School Board*, p. 63.
19. Cox, p. 9.
20. Personal Correspondence, J. M. Frost to T. P. Bell, June 8, 1916.
21. See Robert A. Baker, *A Baptist Source Book* (Nashville: Broadman Press, 1966), pp. 165-168.
22. Frost, p. 82.
23. Ibid.
24. SBC *Annual*, 1912, p. 321.
25. Personal Correspondence, I. J. Van Ness to W. W. Landrum, July 8, 1918.
26. SBC *Annual*, 1891, p. 22.

Isaac Jacobus Van Ness

3 I. J. Van Ness "The Baptist Spirit"

After twenty-five years of service to the Sunday School Board, J. M. Frost died on October 30, 1916. Before his death he went through long weeks of suffering and illness. Letters poured in to his Nashville home from Southern Baptist leaders—Truett, Gambrell, Sampey, and his old friend T. P. Bell.

Frost was born, educated, and married in Kentucky. His first pastorates were in the Bluegrass State. He never lost his love for the region, and he wanted to be buried there. On December 15, 1915, he wrote Cave Hill Cemetery in Louisville, inquiring about burial lots. He made a trip to Louisville and selected a burial spot near the graves of some of the men he most respected in life—James P. Boyce and John A. Broadus.

At his death, newspapers, Baptist and otherwise, exploded with eulogies. The Nashville morning paper said, "For many years he had been the dominating power in the Conventions of the Baptist church." The evening paper said, "He was considered by many the greatest living man in the Baptist church." The *Baptist and Reflector* joined the chorus: "He was probably the most beloved man among Southern Baptists." The *Biblical Recorder* of North Carolina described him as "a great, thoughtful, unselfish, and sagacious leader and administrator."

Dr. Frost's funeral service was in the Broadway Baptist Church in Louisville. Dr. W. W. Landrum, pastor of the church, said in the funeral sermon, "Among all the wise men of the Southern Baptist Convention there was none wiser than he." Allowing for ample exaggeration, these kudos would make any sensitive person pause before following Frost as leader of the Sunday School Board. Who would that person be?

E. Y. Mullins, president of The Southern Baptist Theological Seminary, had participated in the funeral of Frost and had given a personal tribute of praise. A few days after the funeral I. J. Van Ness wrote President Mullins, thanking him for the nice things he had said about Frost. In his response to Van Ness, Mullins wrote, "We are of course greatly interested in his successor, and, confidentially, some of us think you are the man, all of us so far as I know."

But "all" were not sure that Van Ness was the man. His correspondence before and after his election as corresponding secretary documents that fact. As Burroughs said, "there was the concern and misgiving which usually mark the passing of a man tested and trusted and the coming of a man untried."[1] Van Ness—is that a Southern name? a Baptist name? Who was this untested and untried man who refused to campaign for one of the most influential positions in Southern Baptist life? Could he be trusted with so big a job?

The Southern Baptist Convention elected Isaac Jacobus Van Ness as corresponding secretary of the Sunday School Board at the 1917 Convention in New Orleans.[2] In some ways Van Ness was strikingly different from J. M. Frost and T. P. Bell. Frost and Bell were homegrown *Southern* Baptists, Frost from Kentucky and Bell from South Carolina. Van Ness was a Yankee from New Jersey!

Born in East Orange, New Jersey, on July 15, 1860, Van Ness was converted under the preaching of Dr. Edward Judson, son of the great missionary. Although converted in a Baptist church, albeit Northern, Van Ness's first efforts in Christian work were in the interdenominational YMCA ministry. Frost and Bell, in contrast, began and carried out their ministries in a strictly denominational context.

The heritage of Van Ness, as his associate Gaines Dobbins said, "gave to him a breadth of understanding that a born and bred Southern Baptist might not have had."[3] As shall be seen later, Van Ness became *Baptist,* staunch Baptist, staunch *Southern* Baptist! Yet he exuded as cordial a spirit toward other denominations as any Southern Baptist of his time. In fact, in an era when many Southern Baptists were making decidedly Landmarkist and isolationist noises, Van Ness bootlegged a tinge of ecumenism into a BYPU study course book! It was only a tinge, however.

There was another difference in Van Ness and his predecessors, and that was temperament. If Frost was a visionary and Bell a fighter, Van Ness was more of a quiet, conservative scholar. He was neither the Baptist dogmatist of a J. M. Frost nor the Baptist apologist of a T. P. Bell, though he worked with and appreciated both. Hight Moore, who worked with Van Ness at the Board from 1917 until 1935, said that Van Ness's leadership was never spectacular, but "safe and sane and successful." The intelligentsia respected him; the common people heard him gladly.

While Van Ness was different in some ways from Frost and Bell, he also had similarities with them. One thing which all three held in common was the influence of John A. Broadus. Broadus had supported Frost's dream at Fort Worth in 1890 and at Birmingham in 1891. Bell had studied with Broadus at Southern Seminary. After sensing that God had called him to preach, Van Ness enrolled at Southern Seminary because of a sermon he heard Dr. Broadus preach. Van Ness never tired of giving praise to Broadus for the great preacher's influence on his life.

In fact, Van Ness landed in Nashville because of Broadus. One day, while Van Ness was a student at the seminary, Broadus asked him to remain after class. Broadus then introduced him to Dr. W. R. L. Smith, pastor of First Church, Nashville. Smith had gone to the seminary in search of a pastor for the new Immanuel Baptist Church in Nashville. Van Ness went to Nashville, was ordained by First Church, and spent six years, 1890-96, as pastor of Immanuel Baptist Church.

Camaraderie was a second similarity of the first three leaders of the Board. From May 1, 1893, to January 30, 1896, all three men were in Nashville and all had some relationship to the Board. During that period Bell was corresponding secretary; Frost was pastor of First Baptist Church and president (chairman) of the Board; Van Ness was pastor at Immanuel, member of the Board, and editor of *Young People's Leader.* When Bell resigned from the Board in 1896, Van Ness went to Georgia with him as joint editor of the *Christian Index.* But when Samuel Boykin died in 1899, Frost, now corresponding secretary for the second time, enticed Van Ness away from Bell to serve as editorial secretary of the Sunday School Board. That was the position he held when Frost died.

For the first forty-four years (1891-1935) of its life, the Board was in the hands of three men who knew each other well. They had common aims while making distinct and individual contributions to the life of the Board. And that leads to the third common feature of this early triumvirate: Each was energetically committed to the life and ministry of the Sunday School Board. Each of these men saw the potential of the Board as an educational institution for Bible teaching and Christian training, as a missionary "Board" for evangelism, and as a denominational agency for unifying independent churches.

Was Van Ness prepared for the task? What did he bring to the position? From his early years he brought breadth of heritage to the Sunday School Board. From his association with Broadus and Southern Seminary he brought commitment to educational excellence. From the pastorate he brought awareness of local church needs. From conversations with denominational leaders in Nashville and Atlanta, he brought, according to E. Y. Mullins, an unrivaled ability to discern the mood of the Convention. From his editorship of *Young People's Leader* and the *Christian Index* and from his time as editorial secretary of the Board, he brought twenty-two years of publication experience. "Seldom did any man receive more varied and exacting preparation for a surpassingly difficult task."[5]

J. B. Gambrell, who initially opposed the Sunday School Board, in time became one of its staunchest supporters. He was president of the Southern Baptist Convention when Van Ness was elected to lead the Board. Gambrell attended the annual meeting of the Board after the election of Van Ness. Asking no questions and making no suggestions, Gambrell sat through the meeting, observing Van Ness. When Gambrell returned to his home in Texas after the meeting, he said to his friends, "The Sunday School Board has a secretary." Gambrell's assessment became a widespread opinion among Southern Baptist leaders.

If the Sunday School Board now had a secretary, what *kind* of secretary did the organization have? One-word biographies of Van Ness would go like this: quiet; efficient; stately; gentlemanly; educated; conservative. In researching the life of Van Ness, you will not find him to be the kind of person around whom a lot of stories generated. You are more likely to be reminded of the high school principal, proper and serious, yet sensitive.

I. J. Van Ness was essentially an *educator* who was driven to become an *administrator*. Those two words, education and administration, give description to his secretaryship. The Sunday School Board may never have had a more scholarly leader than Van Ness. But it was during his years that administration also emerged as a dominant daily function of the Board's chief executive.

VAN NESS: The Educator

To say that Van Ness was a scholar is fair and accurate. But he was not a scholar's scholar. He did not write technical tomes for university scholars. He was a "scholar" for local Baptist churches. He was an educational broker, one whose ministry was aimed at the person in the pew. But he was an educator!

Gaines Dobbins said that Van Ness "realized that the Sunday School must be made *educationally respectable* if it was to fulfill its mission."[6]

Van Ness demonstrated his desire for educational respectability by the people he selected to work with him. On June 12, 1917, he sent a terse telegram which read:

> You were today elected editor
> Salary thirty three hundred dollars
> Will write.
>
> I. J. Van Ness

That telegram was sent to E. C. Dargan, pastor of First Baptist Church, Macon, Georgia, and one of the most respected personalities in Southern Baptist life. A former president of the Southern Baptist Convention (1911-1913), Dargan had also distinguished himself as a professor of preaching for fifteen years (1892-1907) at The Southern Baptist Theological Seminary. By the time he joined the Board, Dargan was an established authority in the fields of ecclesiology (study of the church) and the history of preaching.

In 1918 Van Ness formed what he called the Editorial Council. He chaired the council, composed of "educationally respectable" people: E. C. Dargan, Hight C Moore, Landrum P. Leavell, and Gaines S. Dobbins. All of those became special names in Southern Baptist history. Van Ness had an eye for quality!

Van Ness wanted quality people to share the educational goal he had. In a Founder's Day Address at the Board in May 1967, Gaines Dobbins remembered some history under the rubric of "They Shared Not the Spotlight: But Helped Build the Board." Dobbins recalled a conversation with Van Ness:

> Dr. Van Ness said to me, in one of our many long talks about the Board, "I am not especially impressed with these figures of sales and receipts. My concern is that so many of our churches have no adequate plans and facilities for teaching the Bible, training their members, and reaching the lost. *Our business is not to*

E. C. Dargan

Hight C Moore

Landrum P. Leavell

Gaines S. Dobbins

40

sell merchandise but to help those churches."[7]

Van Ness was an educator who embodied what he himself called "the Baptist spirit." Historic Baptist life, according to Van Ness, consisted of three things: (1) Baptist principles, (2) the Baptist spirit, and (3) Baptist purposes. He wanted Southern Baptists to safeguard their distinctives, which he believed were the authority of Scripture, the personal nature of faith, the nonsacramental nature of baptism and the Lord's Supper, congregational church life, the equality of all believers, and the separation of church and state. Van Ness believed that attention to those principles would produce a "certain temper of mind," what he called "the Baptist spirit." That spirit was characterized, according to Van Ness, by loyalty to Christ, knowledge of the Bible, an intelligent faith, a sense of personal obligation in matters public and private, and respect for the religious opinions of others. Baptist principles, Van Ness argued, practiced in the Baptist spirit, would produce two great Baptist purposes: evangelism and education.

I. J. Van Ness was a man of unusual balance in religious matters, and he injected that balance into the life of the Sunday School Board. He balanced the lordship of Jesus and the authority of Scripture. "The Lordship of Jesus" was "the fundamental Baptist principle," but another fundamental principle was the sufficiency and authority of the Bible. "We do not put the Bible above Christ, but it is through the Bible we learn of him and know of his teachings,"[8] said Van Ness. Through the ministry of the Sunday School Board, he wanted to help Southern Baptists become a Bible-knowing people, a Bible-loving people, and a Bible-reverencing people.

Van Ness also held in careful balance the tasks of evangelism and education. He would not have one set over against the other, as would some Baptists of his day. And so he would insist that the person who does not believe in an aggressive missionary undertaking is untrue to the Baptist name. But another point needed to be made just as energetically, and Van Ness did not hesitate to make it: "To make men disciples, which is a part of the Commission, and to teach them all things that we have been commanded, we must educate, and this is the Commission just as truly as the command to evangelize."[9]

Just about the time that Van Ness assumed the reins of the Sunday School Board, ecumenism became a hotly debated issue among Southern Baptists. While Van Ness was a devoted denominationalist, again he manifested a balance between what he called "broad sympathy—earnest loyalty." Van Ness stressed the name of Christ and a great desire to be at one with others in discovering the mind of Christ.

This "broad sympathy," however, did not necessitate organic connections between denominations or agencies of those denominations. In 1919 he enunciated four principles the Board would follow in the midst of ecumenical pressures. First, Southern Baptists should maintain control of their own Sunday School work. Second, the Board would not give any interdenominational agency sanction to approach Southern Baptist Sunday Schools. Third, while individuals and churches might properly be related to interdenominational agencies, a denominational agency such as the Board could not do so. Fourth, the Board believed "most heartily in the closest sympathetic relationships with all who are engaged in Sunday School work."

So while Van Ness insisted on "earnest loyalty" to denominational distinctives and warned against an uncritical involvement in ecumenical matters, he also steered the Board away from a policy of exaggerated isolationism. For example, Van Ness "threw all the weight of his position and influence in favor of cooperation"[10] with the Uniform Lesson Committee and the interdenominational International Council on Religious Education. He therefore helped to keep Southern Baptists in the middle of national and worldwide Sunday School work.

As early as 1914 Van Ness had written that "one of the difficult places in the manifestation of the Baptist Spirit" is how to be strict with ourselves and yet tolerant of other people. He wrote in words that continue to be relevant: "As we respect our own Christian life, so must we have respect for every other man in whom we see this same life, for it is God who gave us what we have, and it is God who gives the other man what he has.''[11]

So Van Ness incarnated "the Baptist spirit" at the Board with his sense of spiritual balance. He balanced religious authority by stressing the lordship of Christ and the authority of Scripture. He balanced the mission of the church by stressing evangelism *and* education. He also balanced denominational loyalty with interdenominational cooperation.

But this Baptist educator balanced two other crucial factors for the Board in particular and Southern Baptists in general. He balanced congregationalism with denominational cooperation, and he balanced denominational control of the Board with the mission and integrity of the Board. As to the first—local congregationalism and denominational cooperation—Van Ness believed this to be "our denominational problem." He acknowledged that it was a mystery to many how Baptists could carry on cooperative work within a congregational system of church order. Cooperation can never be compelled, only requested. Van Ness argued that in the tasks of missions, education, and publishing, Baptists would be ineffective apart from combining resources. The combination, however, never diminished the independence of local churches.

One balancing act which every leader of the Board has had to execute is how to maintain the mission and integrity of the Board while acknowledging denominational control over the Board. Maybe no Board leader has done that better than Van Ness. The issue became acute for Van Ness at the point of the Board's "surplus funds." Almost from the beginning of its history the question was raised and agitated regarding what should be done by the Board with the money which exceeded expenses. While the Board had an enviable record of giving funds to other denominational causes such as missions and theological education, some Southern Baptists were willing to let the Board "pick up the tab" for almost all denominational expenses. That is exactly why one of the last things J. M. Frost said to a small group of his co-workers at the Board was, "Brethren, when I am gone please stand guard and do not let the brethren raid the Sunday School Board.''[12]

In the first year of Van Ness's leadership of the Board, he thought, and with good reason, that some wanted to "raid the Board." A resolution was presented to the Convention in 1917 asking the Sunday School Board to consider undertaking all of the administrative expenses of the Home and the Foreign Mission Boards! The next year the Board responded through its secretary. Van Ness argued that such a policy was not only contrary to sound administrative principles, but that it would threaten the stability and mission of the Board itself.

In responding to this request Van Ness also enunciated the principle of trusteeism, a principle as important for all other agencies of the SBC as for the Sunday School Board. The principle, simply stated, says that while the Convention "owns" its agencies and even "determines" policies, the elected members of the Board should be trusted to carry out policies. With regard to surplus funds, Van Ness pled for the Board to have "the final word." In other words, he thought it violated the principle of trusteeism for the administrative policies of the Board to be dictated from the floor of the Southern Baptist Convention. The statement of principles submitted by Van Ness was approved by the Convention in 1918.

That Van Ness was stating principles rather than simply protecting the treasury of the Board is clear by the Board's actions under him. He continued the policy, initiated by Frost, of using surplus funds for other denominational causes. In fact, one wonders what Southern Baptists would have done apart from the generosity of the Board!

When the SBC met in Louisville, Kentucky, in 1927, the Sunday School Board presented a survey of its work for the previous ten years. Those were the first ten years of Van Ness's leadership of the Board. One part of the Board's 1927 report to the Convention was under the heading: "The Sunday School Board Not a Money Hoarding Agency." The figures used to document that assertion are impressive! In 1917 the Board gave $179,201.47 of its earnings to denominational work. In 1927 the Board gave $444,028.41 to denominational causes. From 1891 until 1917 the Board appropriated $965,559.64 to denominational benevolences and missions; from 1917 until 1927 the figure was $2,673,250.18![13]

In his attempt to educate Baptists in "the Baptist spirit," Van Ness also wanted to educate Southern Baptists as to the generosity and mission of the Sunday School Board. The Board had been magnanimous in supporting denominational causes. Southern Baptists, however, had to learn not to "raid the Board" if the Board was to carry out its particular mission for the Convention.

VAN NESS: The Administrator

Frost had dreamed the dream of the Board. Bell had defended it. But Van Ness intensified the quality of the dream. He "educated" the dream by saturating it with "the Baptist spirit." But he also had to administer this burgeoning dream. Like those who would follow him in the office, Van Ness had to organize the ministry of the Sunday School Board so that the educational functions of the Board would have maximum effectiveness.

Van Ness was a gentle administrator. But gentleness should not be mistaken for allowing laziness. One of the most intriguing pieces of correspondence in the Board's history is a letter from Marion Phelps, a devoted worker at the Board, to Van Ness. It is an intercession on behalf of "the folks downstairs." These were the people who worked downstairs in the old Frost Building in the shipping department. It is a moving request to relieve the workers from working Christmas morning! It is too good to edit or paraphrase. The following is a complete copy, dated December 15, 1916, while Van Ness was acting corresponding secretary.

Dear Dr. Van Ness:

I want to make a proposition in behalf of the folks downstairs, and I am making it this way because there is so little opportunity for *talking*.

Probably the heads of the departments do not know how much disappointment is caused by the decision to work Christmas morning. I happen to know of sev-

eral who planned to spend Christmas out of town. Miss Harriet was counting greatly on spending the day with Wilson and his family; Miss Luvell's home is in the country and she planned to go home. Mr. Cravens has not been with his own people on Christmas for a number of years, and was planning to go. One's *own* people mean so much at Christmas.

I think if you talked with any of these they would say they would gladly work at night if they could have the day.

My proposition is this: I will gladly work with them for as many nights as are necessary, and as late as is necessary. Of course I do not understand all the work downstairs, but I am sure there is work I could do, and if they can have their Christmas I will be very glad to do it.[14]

Sincerely,

Marion Phelps

Apparently no one could accuse the Board employees of indolence or Van Ness of being a soft touch!

Of all the corresponding secretaries of the Sunday School Board, probably only James L. Sullivan administered the Board during more difficult days than did I. J. Van Ness. One month before Van Ness was elected by the Convention the country entered World War I. The work of the Board was "sorely taxed and in some measure demoralized" by the war drain. During Van Ness's latter years at the Board, financial panic and depression ravaged the country. The scene was not any better denominationally than it was nationally. Ecumenism and Fundamentalism perplexed the SBC, as did the failure of the 75 Million Campaign. While the Board felt the impact of all these events, Van Ness managed to expand the dream of J. M. Frost.

First, there was an expansion of the internal operations of the Board. On first glance this internal expansion may appear to be little more than the multiplication of bureaucratic structures. Nothing could be further from the truth! Behind and beneath each new development at the Board was a vital ministry needed by the churches and people of the SBC.

Under Frost the Nashville Board had been,

Top: Accounting Department, ca. 1935

Bottom: The church literature mailing room, ca. 1897

Nashville Baptist Book Store, ca. 1927

as Robert A. Baker said, "little more than an editorial office where Frost, Van Ness, and Burroughs prepared the literature, filled the orders, and received reports."[15] The remaining Board employees were field secretaries, dispersed across the Convention. In summary, the Board was loosely organized, relatively simple and with limited focus.

Under Van Ness, however, a "radical transformation" in the Board's structure occurred. Here began the official departmentalization of the Board. In 1917 the business aspects of the Board were placed in three new departments: (1) Bookkeeping and Cashier's Department, (2) Order and Mailing Department, and (3) Sales Department.

By 1919 five other departments had been added: (1) the Editorial Department under the superb leadership of E. C. Dargan and Hight C Moore, (2) The Organized Class Department under H. L. Strickland, (3) the BYPU Department under Landrum P. Leavell, (4) the Missionary Publications Department under Gaines S. Dobbins, and (5) the Church Architecture Department under Prince E. Burroughs.

45

Each of these five departments reflected something significant about the life of the Board. The Editorial Department, which Van Ness once described as "the heart of all our activities," prepared the denomination's religious literature. The Organized Class Department, as well as the BYPU Department, signaled the denominationalizing of inter-denominational movements. Gaines S. Dobbins's ministry suggested that the Board was a part of the missions enterprise, a cherished emphasis of T. P. Bell. Also, the Church Architecture Department represented a response to an urgent need in Southern Baptist life. Baptist church houses, like all others, had been built for corporate worship, not education for smaller groups. This department helped to make sure that there was a "place" for the Sunday School.

One area in which the Board never created a department but made an incalculable contribution was the development of rural churches. Always a concern of the Board, the revitalization of rural congregations through active, well-organized Sunday Schools received new attention beginning in 1918. Working with state convention boards, the Sunday School Board made available both personnel and funds for this strategic ministry.

In 1922 the Convention appointed a "Country Church Commission" to make a comprehensive study of conditions of country churches in the SBC. Van Ness chaired the commission and E. P. Alldredge of the Board made the study. The report, issued in 1924,

indicated that 88.5 percent of all SBC churches were rural and contained 68 percent of total SBC membership. Trained leaders and pastors, modern church buildings, larger and better organized Sunday School and BYPU departments were listed as "imperative needs." Increasing financial appropriations came from the Board for rural work. In 1928 alone the Board contributed over $81,000 for this purpose. This commitment to the development and renewal of country churches is a good example of the "hidden history" of the Board. And it is the history of a ministry to meet a need. No statistical listing, no matter how massive or impressive, could ever document the value of such ministry.

The internal expansion of the Board's ministries continued under Van Ness. Ever since the first issue of *Kind Words,* the Christian nurture of children and young people had been central. In 1919 Lilian S. Forbes came from Alabama to head the newly established Elementary Department. Highlighting the

E. P. Alldredge

46

need for the moral development of young people, the Board also created the Vacation Bible School Department. Dr. Homer L. Grice, pastor of the First Baptist Church of Washington, Georgia, inaugurated the VBS Department in 1924. Calling for good stewardship in the use of church facilities as well as help for the young, Grice spelled out the purpose of the new Department:

The purpose of the department is to get the churches to use their idle Sunday school plants in the summer months . . . and give them [the children] a daily three-hour program of teaching that will minister to their physical, mental, social, moral, and spiritual needs.[16]

Emphasis upon youth continued with the formation of the Intermediate Department under Mary Virginia Lee and the Department of Student Work under Frank H. Leavell and William Hall Preston.

Two early leaders of the Department of Student Work were Frank H. Leavell (below left) and William Hall Preston (right).

Left: Homer L. Grice began the VBS Department in 1924.

Above: Homer and Ethel Grice

47

One of the most famous names in the annals of the Board is Arthur Flake. A layman, traveling salesman, and department store manager, Flake became so successful as a volunteer Sunday School superintendent in his home church of Winona, Mississippi, that he was elected a field worker for the Board in 1909. His primary contribution to the Christian education of Southern Baptists came as head of the Sunday School Administration Department, organized in 1920 at the Board. In this position "he developed, standardized, and popularized a philosophy and methodology of Sunday school organization and administration"[17] on which much of Southern Baptist Sunday School growth was based. The famous "Flake's Formula" for building a Sunday School consisted of five steps: (1) take a census to find the people, (2) enlarge the organization, (3) train the workers, (4) provide a place, and (5) visit the prospects.

What Arthur Flake meant for Sunday School expansion, John L. Hill meant for the expansion of the book publishing ministry of the Board. Hill, a former dean at Georgetown College in Kentucky, assumed the leadership

Above: Arthur Flake

Right: John L. Hill

of the Book Publishing Department, organized in 1922, at the Board. Under him this aspect of the Board's ministry became increasingly important.

Hill is also the one responsible for the naming of Broadman Press. Baptists of the North had long used the famous Baptist missionary name of Judson as their publication press name. Hill wanted Southern Baptists to have such a name. In the jubilee history of the Sunday School Board, P. E. Burroughs provides an account of how Hill settled in 1933 on the name of Broadman:

> For ten years, Dr. Hill, the book editor, and others with him considered the matter; many phrases were proposed, but none seemed quite acceptable. In July, 1933, Dr. Hill was entering Greenville, South Carolina, aboard a Pullman. He was pondering the question of a press name which might be significant and at the same time acceptable to the Southern people. As he entered Greenville, he was thinking of the earlier publishing board and the immortal fathers who projected that antecedent of the present Sunday School Board, John A. Broadus who was the secretary and Basil Manly who was the president. While he was shaving in the dressing room of the Pullman, like a flash came the inspiration, why not honor these men and in so doing honor ourselves by blending into one the first syllable of their names? Why not *Broadman Press?*[18]

George W. Card

Noble Van Ness

That day he wrote a letter to Noble Van Ness, son of the corresponding secretary but also managing editor of the Board, urging the adoption of "Broadman" after the "two near patron saints" of Southern Baptists.

It was not enough, however, to publish books under a satisfactory press name; some method had to be devised to circulate the books. Under I. J. Van Ness's leadership a program of cooperation between the Sunday School Board and the various state mission boards was initiated for distributing books. This was the beginning of the Baptist Book Stores, now operated by the Board. In 1924 George W. Card, minister of music and education at Walnut Street Baptist Church in Louisville, Kentucky, became manager of the Advertising Department at the Board. The advertising and sale of books became a major part of his responsibility.

Two other departments developed under Van Ness. One was the Department of Survey, Statistics, and Information. A growing denominational life demanded an orderly collection of statistical and historical information. Established in 1921 and initially led by E. P. Alldredge, this department has helped Southern Baptists to understand themselves. The Department of Church Administration, begun in 1927, was designed to meet the needs of pastors, other staff members, deacons, and general church workers. *Church Administration*, a monthly magazine, was immediately launched to help meet needs of church organization, finances, and related matters.

Above: Shipping Building

Left: Pritchell Hall
           at Ridgecrest, ca. 1920

This vast expansion of the ministries of the Board naturally required more physical space. The Frost Building had been dedicated in only 1914, and most had considered this a spacious accommodation for years to come. They were underexpecting! By 1919 two stories had to be added to the building which had been expected to serve for decades. In 1923 the Board reported to the Convention that a six-story shipping building had been constructed on Ninth Avenue and a two-story printing building had been erected on Commerce Street.

The Board was expanding not only internally, in terms of ministries offered and buildings constructed. As stated earlier, it continued to expand its support of other denominational efforts. For example, the Board helped to spearhead the establishment of the Annuity Board of the SBC by setting aside $100,000 for beginning a fund for ministerial relief. In response to Convention request the Board cooperated in supporting the beginning of the New Orleans Baptist Theological Seminary and appropriated funds for the work of the Education Commission. When the SBC launched the Five-Year Campaign (1919-1924) to raise $75,000,000, the Board provided housing for the campaign, acted as fiscal agent, and undergirded the effort in every way.

Few, if any, programs of the SBC failed to receive the solid support of the Board. It contributed financially to the Committee on Baptist History, forerunner to the Historical Commission; the Layman's Missionary Movement, forerunner to the Brotherhood Commission; and the Social Service Commission, forerunner to the Christian Life Commission. The Executive Committee and the Baptist World Alliance were also beneficiaries of the Sunday School Board. In a very real sense, the life of the Sunday School Board has been one with the life of the Southern Baptist Convention. The role of the Board as "institutional philanthropist" to Southern Baptists has never been fully recognized. And behind all of this work was the administrative hand of I. J. Van Ness.

Perhaps more importantly than funding Southern Baptist causes during the Van Ness years of 1917-1935, the Sunday School Board continued to help forge the denominational identity of Southern Baptists. By standardizing educational organization and methodology, as well as by furnishing the churches a common literature for Sunday School, Training Union, and Vacation Bible School, the Board helped to shape a uniform church life within the Convention. In 1919 the Board initiated a "Denominational Day" for the promotion of denominational principles and programs. The SBC approved the idea and suggested an annual observance. The Student Department helped to create and sustain Southern Baptist loyalty and a denominational spirit among future leaders of the SBC.

While the 75 Million Campaign and the Cooperative Program were primary factors in developing the sense of financial stewardship among Southern Baptist individuals and churches, the work of the Board should not be overlooked. "Financing the Kingdom" through tithing became a recurring emphasis of the Board's periodical literature and books. Stewardship promotion was a dominant theme of the Board in the 1920s. The first tract issued by the Department of Church Administration dealt with the subject of stewardship. Tithing became a characteristic emphasis of Southern Baptists, largely due to the Sunday School Board.

While the Board was reluctant to do so, it gradually assumed financial and program responsibility for Ridgecrest Baptist Assembly in Ridgecrest, North Carolina. A summer encampment, Ridgecrest had struggled for survival since the time it was chartered in 1907. The Sunday School Board guaranteed the continuation of Ridgecrest. The Board made it clear in 1935, however, that its purpose in conducting the Assembly was "to relate it to the life of the denomination, and not to develop it simply as a hotel or summer resort." Whatever the Board touched—denominational or interdenominational—during the Van Ness years, it thoroughly "Southern Baptistized" it.

As one would expect, the life of the Board was not exempt from criticism. It was not exempt in its beginning years, its middle years, or its later years. After drawing some fire for material appearing in periodicals, the Board adopted an editorial policy in 1930 which may have forfeited some leadership role for the sake of keeping the denominational peace. A part of this policy stated "that the work of the Sunday School Board should be constructive and for the promotion of the generally established views of our denomination, and that all articles should conserve this principle." The policy went on to say "that our writers shall avoid the discussion of questions, at any time, which are unsettled, and the occasion of sharp issues among our people."[18] So if, under Van Ness, the Board was shaping the denomination, which it surely was, the Convention was also shaping the Board. Traffic ran both ways!

When I. J. Van Ness retired in 1935, an era had passed in the life of the Board. He had worked with both Frost and Bell, had witnessed the Board as a fledgling institution, and had been instrumental in its maturation. No one has described the early years of the Sunday School Board under Van Ness better than Noble Van Ness, the corresponding secretary's son. Noble worked at the Board for forty-three years, from 1922 until 1965, and he knew the amusing idiosyncrasies and unbelievable gifts of that early band of laborers. In a few pages on the early history of the Board, he uncovered some of its life.

Mitchell E. Dunaway was the Board's first purchasing agent. Noble Van Ness described the bald-headed, tightfisted Dunaway with the following words:

M. E. Dunaway

In 1891 M. E. Dunaway wrapped the first package of Board literature. His temperament was such that he would have wrapped the last one if possible. He was of the old school that kept their counsel, their reasons, and their business knowledge strictly to themselves. To this day I do not know how he decided on the quantities of each periodical to offer, except NEVER too many. . . . The most

he ever said on this subject was a crisp, "Throw away—go away." Which meant that no one who threw anything away could stay with him.

I can see him now in shirt sleeves and long dark green canvas apron addressing labels by hand, putting them on packages and sorting them to mail sacks, and saying nothing. . . . He knew what he was doing, but the rest of us only knew that his part of the team work would go off quietly, correctly, properly, and on time.

Noble Van Ness remembered E. C. Dargan as "the fiery little mustached editor from South Carolina." "If he had been old enough in 1861," Noble said of Dargan, "he would have captured Fort Sumter by the heat of his temper." And then comes the tribute: "But a more cultured gentleman never lived. I loved him devotedly and admired his keen intellect immensely. To me he will always be that knight of the Old South at its best."

In the early years of I. J. Van Ness's leadership at the Board, the organization was simple. It consisted more of people who knew one another than of procedures to follow. By the end of Van Ness's time, that had changed somewhat. But in three brief paragraphs Noble Van Ness recalled the earliest years, who was respected, what the working conditions were, and the shape of the personalities:

The organization was a simple one of people, not procedures. The field workers were always working in the churches instead of holding "Why Am I Here?" At-Home Weeks in Nashville. Editors were a special breed. They represented brains and class and were looked up to by the churches. The rest of us were just around.

We were around six days a week, by the way, from eight to five, except that we wasted Saturday afternoon by going home. This was slightly suspect as being against God's will. And who ever heard of air-conditioning, pension plans, job descriptions, evaluations, or salary scales?

Dunaway ruled the order and mailing in his separate world. We had no worries there nor any chance to have them.

B. W. Spilman, the first field secretary, would occasionally bounce into Nashville like a fat little Brer Rabbit. Prince Emmanuel Burroughs whistled through his dentures as he talked on church architecture. John L. Hill edited books, without ever editing manuscripts, between audience-moving speaking engagements. L. P. Leavell lived B.Y.P.U. George Card took care of advertising and had a hard time getting periodical cover pages away from editor Hight C Moore.

The Lord must have been with us, for we grew like topsy.

"Grew like Topsy!" That's what the Sunday School Board did under I. J. Van Ness. By 1935, however, Van Ness was seventy-five years old and declining in health and leadership ability. He had secured himself a place in the "royal line." But now new leadership was needed. It came out of Mississippi by way of Oklahoma City, and it was pastoral in nature.

Notes

1. P. E. Burroughs, *Fifty Fruitful Years,* p. 173.
2. Until 1924 the corresponding secretary of any SBC Board was elected by the SBC. After 1924 the Boards elected their own chief executives.
3. Gaines S. Dobbins, *Great Teachers Make a Difference* (Nashville: Broadman Press, 1965), p. 68.
4. Ibid., pp. 70-71.
5. Burroughs, *Fifty Fruitful Years,* p. 173.
6. Dobbins, *Great Teachers,* p. 74. Underlining mine.
7. Underlining mine.
8. I. J. Van Ness, *The Baptist Spirit* (Nashville: The Sunday School Board of the Southern Baptist Convention, 1914), p. 23.
9. Ibid., p. 22.
10. Dobbins, p. 76.
11. Van Ness, p. 65.
12. B. W. Spilman, "James Marion Frost: Memories," an unpublished manuscript in Dargan-Carver Library, p. 11.
13. SBC *Annual,* 1927, p. 333.
14. This letter is with the Van Ness Papers, Dargan-Carver Library.
15. Robert A. Baker, *The Story of the Sunday School Board* (Nashville: Convention Press, 1966), p. 97.
16. As quoted in Burroughs, *Fifty Fruitful Years,* p. 214.
17. *Encyclopedia of Southern Baptists* (Nashville: Broadman Press, 1958), vol. I, p. 441.
18. SBC *Annual,* 1930, p. 303.

Hight C Moore at his home at Ridgecrest

Thomas Luther Holcomb

4 T. L. Holcomb "To the Last Church"

When T. L. Holcomb (1882-1972) moved to Nashville in 1935 to become executive-secretary of The Sunday School Board of the Southern Baptist Convention, he hung a picture of a small rural church in his office. That act told it all. And it pointed the direction of the Board for the next eighteen years. He would make certain that every possible effort would be made to reach "the last church" in the most remote area of the Southern Baptist Convention.

Who was Thomas Luther Holcomb? The answer is important because what he did as executive-secretary of the Board was rooted in who he was and what he had done. Holcomb was a native Mississippian, thoroughly acquainted with rural and small-church life. Born in Purvis, Mississippi, on December 22, 1882, he was only nine years old when J. M. Frost began the Sunday School Board. His leadership at the Board, therefore, marked a second generation which would build upon foundations already laid.

With only brief interruptions Holcomb remained in Mississippi for the first thirty-nine years of his life. After completing his education at The Southern Baptist Theological Seminary, he served as pastor of churches in Durant, Yazoo City, Pontotoc, and Columbia, Mississippi. His son recalled that Holcomb often "went to rural churches where baptisms were in rivers and streams."[1] Clifton J. Allen, who worked closely with Holcomb at the Board, spoke at Holcomb's funeral in 1972. "He remembered his origin, his beginnings,"[2] said Allen. And he brought a concern for his heritage to the ministry of the Sunday School Board. His work there pulsated with concern to help weak and undeveloped churches.

Frost was a builder. Bell was a fighter. Van Ness was an educator. But T. L. Holcomb was a pastor. His emphasis and style of leadership at the Board were essentially pastoral in nature. After studying the history of the Board under Holcomb, one gets the clear impression that Holcomb perceived the Sunday School Board as "church," employees as "church staff," and himself as "pastor."

Something of that perception was needed when Holcomb became the Board's leader; it was certainly understandable in light of his previous ministry. After serving churches in Mississippi for a number of years, he became pastor of the First Baptist Church of Sherman, Texas, in 1921. In 1928, after seven years at Sherman, he became executive-secretary of the Baptist General Convention of Texas for one year. From 1929 until 1935 he was pastor of the large and influential First Baptist Church of Oklahoma City, Oklahoma. His pastoral experience had provided firsthand knowledge of both small and large churches in the Southern Baptist Convention.

From the pastorate he brought to the Board an unswerving commitment to the Bible as the Word of God. When elected as executive-secretary, Holcomb stood before the messengers at the 1935 meeting of the SBC in Memphis, raised the Bible, and said: "I accept the Bible as the inspired Word of God and pledge that the Sunday School Board will be true to its teachings."[3] Frost, Bell, and Van Ness, as well as Sullivan and Cothen who succeeded Holcomb, have all stood by the same affirmation. But Holcomb had a particular reason for the raised Bible. He had been in Texas and Oklahoma where Frank Norris's angry fundamentalism had questioned the integrity of almost all Southern Baptist institutions. He also knew that the Board itself had come under fire, so he wanted to launch his ministry with a positive confession.

Holcomb also brought from the pastorate the urgency of evangelism. He said "many times that if he thought any denominational position would cause him to lose the spirit of evangelism he would ask the Lord to take him out of it."[4] James L. Sullivan recounted three characteristic emphases of Holcomb:

> First, was his emphasis on the Bible as the revealed Word of God, divinely recorded as God's revelation and guide to man. The second was his emphasis on evangelism, the one hope of the world, the heartbeat that has to be in everything we do and write in every area of the denomination's life and in the local church. His third emphasis was on the local church and its autonomy, but also its importance.[5]

A pastoral style of leadership dominated at the Board during the Holcomb era. He was above all promotional, but he was also inspirational and accessible. The door to his office, so it is said, was kept open so that the employees of the Board, as well as any other Southern Baptist, would feel free to enter. While such a gesture reflected Holcomb's pastoral instincts, it may have also suggested why he "never claimed to be a skilled administrator."[6] Between 350 and 400 people worked at the Board when Holcomb first went there. Compared to the 1,500 who work there in 1981, that is a small number. But an open door for 350 employees would not be considered administrative astuteness! However, when asked how many people worked at the Board, Holcomb would often reply with his typical humor, "About half of them!" Maybe he knew they would not all want in through the open door to his office. Again, however,

his style was pastoral accessibility.

It was also inspirational. By the time Holcomb came to the Board the title had been changed from "corresponding secretary" to "executive-secretary." Neither fit him. He was never the methodical manager of an institution, plotting a course at the drawing board. He blew bugles. With a rapid-fire delivery, he aroused and encouraged and gave hope. Coming to the Board on the heels of depression in the nation and fundamentalism in the denomination, as well as the declining years of Van Ness's leadership in the institution, Holcomb created a new beginning. In his history of the Board published six years after Holcomb arrived, Burroughs described the impact of Holcomb:

> The early days of the new order under Dr. Holcomb witnessed, both at headquarters and on the field, a quickening of spiritual purpose and a strengthening of spiritual fellowship. Along with this development came a speeding up of the machinery, a girding for larger achievement. No special authority was exercised, no com-

P. E. Burroughs, Holcomb, and Hight C Moore

56

mands were issued, seldom was there direct appeal. Rather there grew a new atmosphere, there came a sense of comradeship, there developed a will to win.[7]

E. E. Lee, an early field secretary at the Board, once recalled Holcomb's charismatic and positive leadership. During World War II the Board, like every other institution in American society, was plagued by handicap. Some sacrifice was needed in the midst of uncertainty. So T. L. Holcomb stood before the annual meeting of the Sunday School Board and state workers and proclaimed, "We are going on!"[8] E. E. Lee remembered that everyone present "responded with every desire in our makeup." Holcomb led with his zeal.

Van Ness was most comfortable sitting at a desk, editing a manuscript. Holcomb was more at home before an audience, promoting the multiple ministries of the Board. Each was needed at different periods in the history of the institution. Holcomb did not become a promoter after he came to the Board; he had

always promoted as a pastor. While at First Church, Sherman, Texas, he had one of the largest BYPU organizations west of the Mississippi. His son believed that it was during the Sherman pastorate that his father "developed the reputation for being a denominational person, a genius in Sunday School work, and a great power as an evangelist."[9] If Holcomb was not an administrative genius, he possessed extraordinary promotional gifts.

Most remember his white hair, his neat appearance (including professionally manicured fingernails), and his short stature. He could not see over the average lectern, so he often stood to one side with his arm propped against the stand; or he would move from side to side as he spoke. Though he had an infectious sense of humor and a warm and encouraging personality, he also knew how to be sharp—quickly. He could be tough. Given the position he held, that was a compliment.

By calling, experience, and instinct, Holcomb was a pastor. Committed to the Bible as the Word of God, convinced of the centrality of evangelism, and sensitive to the local church, he brought to the Board the art of promotion under inspirational leadership. He was not a scholar; nor did he possess the editorial or writing abilities of any of his three predecessors. Those who followed him would be more gifted administratively.

Porter Routh worked with Holcomb at the Board before becoming executive-secretary of the Executive Committee of the SBC. When Holcomb died, Routh wrote a column, reflecting on his former boss. In a brief, seven-word sentence, Routh explained Holcomb: "He was always a pastor at heart."[10]

What did this pastor-become-executive-secretary do for eighteen years at the Board? More accurately, what did the Board do under his leadership during those years?

The dominant goal of the Sunday School Board during the Holcomb years was to make available to every church within the Southern Baptist Convention the vast resources of the Board. Van Ness, Frost, and Bell had built up those resources within the Board. Now Holcomb wanted to transport those resources outside the Board. The task was promotional in nature.

Porter Routh, Holcomb, and B. B. McKinney

A. V. Washburn, J. E. Lambdin, J. N. Barnette, and others at the open house of the Tower Building in 1953

Immediately after going to the Board, Holcomb launched a major effort to reach the churches. It was called "The Five-Year Sunday School Board Promotional Program" and more commonly known as simply "The Five-Year Program." On Thanksgiving morning, 1935, only five months after Holcomb went to the Board, the heads of the Sunday School departments met the executive-secretary in a committee room in the Frost Building. They gathered for prayer and consultation. P. E. Burroughs described what happened:

> The burden of their prayer was that they might be led into a fuller fellowship and that God would send them out on some concerted mission worthy of the Sunday School Board and the ministries in which they served. The hours passed, and as they waited in quietness, the idea emerged that they might join their comrades in the various states in a cooperative Southwide effort to "carry from the steps of the Sunday School Board Building to the last church all that we have come to know about Sunday School and Training Union methods." This phrase, carved out by Dr. Holcomb, became the accepted slogan.[11]

From this meeting came the Five-Year Program. It was launched in 1936 and culminated in 1940. A strategy of immense importance for Southern Baptist life in general, and the Board in particular, was developed in the Five-Year Program. The strategy was to use the district associations as the major units for promoting every phase of Sunday School and Training Union work.

While this was not a new idea, associations had never been extensively utilized as channels of denominational promotion. Persons such as Arthur Flake and J. N. Barnette, however, had advocated the concept for over ten years. Under Flake's leadership the Department of Sunday School Administration had published a leaflet in 1924 entitled "Organizing the Association for Sunday School Work." And in 1929, Flake's department presented a report to the SBC which underscored the very strategy used in the Five-Year Program. That 1929 report stated:

> We are stressing everywhere and with all possible emphasis the need of proper associational Sunday school organization. First, as the best and only means of reaching *every* church in the Convention territory with the modern Sunday school program; and second, as the best means of continually promoting the increased effectiveness of the work in all the churches.[12]

This 1929 report of the Sunday School Administration Department sounds very much like a model used by Holcomb and others in inaugurating the Five-Year Program.

But why were the district associations such a valuable channel for reaching the churches? First, and obviously, because the associations were closer to the churches than any other unit in denominational life. By utilizing the associations, all the churches, and not just those with initiative and interest, could be reached. When the Five-Year Program began in 1936, there were 24,537 churches in the Southern Baptist Convention. However, 15,000 of those churches were one-fourth-time churches and 5,000 were one-half-time. In other words, 80 percent of all Southern Baptist churches had less than full-time worship services and undeveloped educational ministries. Good reason existed to try to reach "the last church." The district association, because of proximity to the churches, was the best means for reaching those churches.

A second reason for developing associational Sunday School and Training Union programs was to generate more volunteer workers. A tendency had evolved in the state conventions and the Sunday School Board to employ special workers to promote these programs. But "Dr. Holcomb in his Texas and Oklahoma pastorates and in his ministry as leader of Texas Baptists had developed some rather definite convictions regarding the propriety and even the necessity of depending as largely as possible on voluntary service, both in church work and in general denominational ministry."[13] The Five-Year Program was designed to enlist and train thirty thousand volunteer workers in the work of Sunday School and Training Union.

In the Five-Year Program, the Board worked through the state conventions to reach the associations and through the associations to reach the churches. This method helped to strengthen state conventions by bringing the associations in closer cooperation with the states. In other words, this program of the Board intensified the growing denominational connectionalism between units in Southern Baptist life. It denominationalized!

The execution of the Five-Year Program was relatively simple. The plan called for a two-day Sunday School conference and a two-day Training Union conference in every state of the Southern Baptist Convention for the five-year period. Representatives from all associations in the states were invited to attend. To encourage attendance the Board provided travel expenses for the associational representatives who were to carry the programs back to the associational level and ulti-

W. A. Harrell

mately to the churches. At the Board itself J. N. Barnette directed the Sunday School division of the program, and W. A. Harrell led the Training Union emphasis.

By building upon foundations already laid, Holcomb used the Five-Year Program to launch the most extensive Sunday School and Training Union promotional emphasis ever made by the Board to that time. The statistical results of the Five-Year Program were impressive. In the five-year period of 1936-1940 Sunday School enrollment increased 432,916; Vacation Bible School enrollment increased 400,328; Training Union enrollment increased 250,459. During the same period 1,339 new Sunday Schools and 4,712 new Vacation Bible Schools were established. Also, 2,174 churches added Training Union to their educational ministry.

Robert A. Baker called the Five-Year Program "a watershed in its wide influence." It complemented the evangelistic emphasis of the Southern Baptist Convention. It also gave additional impetus to the planning and programming features of Southern Baptist life.

Moreover, it enhanced the Board's ministry in the several areas of periodical circulation, book distribution, the development of church libraries, and the renewed attention given to improving church buildings. Probably as much as anything else, however, it continued the process, long before begun by the Board, of uniforming Southern Baptist church life. In brief, it helped to etch more clearly the Southern Baptist organizational identity.

The Five-Year Program concluded December 31, 1940. Immediately, however, a new Four-Year Program, looking toward the centennial celebration of the SBC in 1845, was launched. The statistical results of the Five-Year Program are impressive:

	1935	1940	Increase
Number of Sunday Schools	22,883	24,222	1,339
Sunday School Enrollment	3,157,458	3,590,374	432,916
Number of Training Unions (churches with Training Union)	n/a	14,180	
Total Training Union Enrollment	669,230	919,689	250,459
Number of Vacation Bible Schools	1,044	5,756	4,712
Vacation Bible School Enrollment	140,878	541,206	400,328

Holcomb was leading the Board out of one promotional campaign into another! This second promotional effort was built upon the first, though it was to be more intense. Plans called for "separate one-day conferences for the promotion of Sunday school and Training Union work in every association in the Convention" for each of the four years, 1941-1944. Some believed that this would be "the greatest organized promotional effort ever made by any denomination."[14]

It was not to be. World War II crippled this promotional effort, as it did most other aspects of the ministry of the Board. Whether the Board would have been as successful in a second high-powered campaign, even apart from the war, is questionable. There were efforts, however. J. N. Barnette again directed the associational Sunday School emphasis, and Chester L. Quarles served in that capacity in Training Union. But no amount of commitment to the project could withstand the drain of the war. Between 1941 and 1944 both Sunday School and Training Union enrollment declined. Vacation Bible School enrollment, however, continued to show a slight increase.

The Four-Year Program achieved at least one thing, however. By building upon the strategy of the Five-Year Program, it identified the district association as a key factor in the promotion of denominational programs. Indeed, these two programs may have intensified transformation in associational life which was already occurring in Southern Baptist life. Whereas associations became channels of denominational programs to the churches, they had once been advisory bodies responding to needs which came from the churches. In both cases, however, the needs of the churches were paramount. The 1945 report of the Board to the Convention reflected on the success of utilizing the associations and the purpose of the Board in doing so: "It is our purpose to press forward with the full teaching and training ministry of the Board through the associations until we have reached every church and unchurched community."[15] Holcomb had found a handle! He intended to go to "the last church."

While his efforts were stymied because of war, Holcomb saw phenomenal growth in the ministry of the Board following World War II. He had the privilege of riding the crest of a general upswing in the religious life of America in the postwar years. In his final eight years (1945-53) at the Board, Holcomb presided over a mushrooming agency. The expansion of the Board's ministry in those years took place, in the words of Robert A. Baker, "at an unprecedented rate."

Statistics are often cold. But these in the following table burn with postwar advance.

	1945	1953
SS enrollment in the SBC	3,380,630	5,491,056
TU enrollment in the SBC	759,885	1,677,293
Number of VBS in the SBC	7,484	21,741
VBS enrollment in the SBC	635,947	2,059,163
Total receipts of Sunday School Board	$4,157,884	$12,696,200

In this eight-year period, Sunday School enrollment in SBC churches increased over 2,100,000! Training Union enrollment increased more than it had in all the preceding years! The number of Vacation Bible Schools among Southern Baptists had almost tripled! And the total receipts of the Sunday School Board had more than tripled!

Even in the midst of a general religious boom, this is an impressive record. Surely a burgeoning economy and the spiritual hunger following the war go far in explaining this "stat sheet." Much of this growth would have occurred no matter who was executive-secretary of the Board. But much of it is due to the promotional parson in the person of T. L. Holcomb. The times were tuned to the man; the man was made for the times.

During his tenure, Holcomb did more than promote the staple educational programs of Sunday School and Training Union. He, and those who labored with him, instigated new ministries. Some of these ministries were begun in response to requests of the Convention; others were initiated by the Board itself.

One of Holcomb's first objectives when he went to the Board was to emphasize church music. As far back as Manly and Broadus, the Board had manifested an interest in hymnology and church music. A number of song-books and hymnals had been published,[16] but no department had been organized within the Board to promote church music. Holcomb would see to its formation.

As a pastor he had known the power of music in the ministry of the church. Holcomb's son recalled an incident in his father's ministry at Oklahoma City when the singing of hymns played a big part. It occurred during the depression, and suicides were common. Luther Holcomb reported it this way:

> One day my father took me along with him to see the city manager. As soon as he saw my father in the reception room he said, "Come on in, Preacher. You've come down here to talk about the suicides, and there is nothing I can do about them." My father told him that he wanted permission to go on the streets of Oklahoma City after the Sunday evening services. "I don't want to preach. I want a truck, and I want a choir, and I want that choir to sing hymns like How Firm a Foundation, Blessed Assurance, and Amazing Grace. All I want to do is stand up on the back of that truck and read verses such as 'God is our refuge and strength, a very present help in trouble.' "[17]

B. B. McKinney leading music
at Ridgecrest, ca. 1941

The city manager approved, and the pastor persuaded his church choir to sing on the back of a truck on the streets of the city.

B. B. McKinney was one of the first persons Holcomb added to the Sunday School Board staff. As music editor, McKinney was to help "produce and promote . . . the right kind of music" for Southern Baptist churches. McKinney went to the Board after serving on the music faculty at Southwestern Baptist Theological Seminary. He had also been an assistant pastor at Travis Avenue Baptist Church in Fort Worth, Texas.

In his first report to the Convention, McKinney described his purpose at the Board: "to magnify *Heart Music* for the masses through associational and statewide conferences."[18] He was the author of the words and music of 149 gospel hymns. Some of his best remembered are "The Nail-Scarred Hand," "Let Others See Jesus in You," "Speak to My Heart," and "Wherever He Leads I'll Go."

McKinney edited and the Sunday School Board published *The Broadman Hymnal* in 1940. This became the most widely used hymn book in Southern Baptist churches, and it helped to standardize worship and hymnody among Southern Baptists. Other than the Bible, this hymnal was Southern Baptists' only "Book of Common Prayer." Two later hymn books published by the Board would continue to function in that capacity.

Under McKinney's leadership, the Sunday School Board created a Department of Church Music in 1941. McKinney, as the first secretary of that department, began an annual Church Music Week at Ridgecrest in 1941, developed a Church Music Training Course in 1946, and launched a new magazine, *The Church Musician,* in 1950. In 1944 the Board fostered the development of church music in the state conventions by offering to pay one-third of the salary of any well-qualified, full-time state music secretary.

McKinney died in 1952 as the result of an automobile accident while returning from Music Week at Ridgecrest. He was succeeded as secretary of the Church Music Department by W. Hines Sims. In bringing McKinney to the Board, T. L. Holcomb indirectly made a major contribution to the worship practices of Southern Baptist churches.

Under Holcomb's direction the Board assumed other new programs designed to serve the churches of the SBC. A Church Library Service was established by the Board in 1943. Florida Waite directed this program, which had roots reaching back to the early life of the Board. An effort at capitalizing on audiovisual aids for local church education was made in 1943 when the Board began the Visual Education Service. Norman O'Neal became director in 1944. By 1951 this service had developed into a department of the Board, and Earl Waldrup became secretary. Also, in 1943 the Board authorized a service known as the Christian Recreation Service, the beginning of the Church Recreation Department.[19]

Recognizing a need to minister to the family in the postwar years, the Board created a Department of Home Curriculum in December 1945. Beginning the next month, Joe Burton served as editor of the department; and in January 1947, he began editing *Home Life,* a monthly Christian family magazine.

In 1948 the Board started what has become a "Southern Baptist institution"—the January Bible Study Week. An attempt to supplement the Bible teaching of the Sunday Schools, the January Bible Study was designed as an intensive, one-week study of a book of the Bible by adults and young people under the leadership of the pastor. In that first year of 1948 the book of Ephesians was studied by six thousand churches in the SBC. While that in itself was an enviable number, by 1953 the Board reported that the majority of churches in the SBC were involved in this special week of Bible study. Today the January Bible Study program is one of the most effective means of Christian education in Southern Baptist Churches. Holcomb and associates were finding other handles for reaching the churches!

Another major development under Holcomb was the establishment of Glorieta Baptist Assembly in Glorieta, New Mexico. Ridgecrest in North Carolina had made immeasurable contributions to Southern Baptist life. But the western constituency of the SBC was increasing. No one was more aware of this than the former pastor of First Church,

Pioneer Week at Glorieta, 1952

Oklahoma City. After the SBC had appointed a committee in 1947 to study the possibility of a western assembly and after the Convention chose Glorieta as the site, the Sunday School Board was charged by the Convention to develop and operate the new assembly. T. L. Holcomb had led in projecting the assembly, and in 1952 the first conferences were held at Glorieta. Most of the development of Glorieta would come under Holcomb's successor, but Southern Baptists are indebted to Holcomb for his role in leading the way.

When Holcomb began his work at the Board, the Board had just over 350 employees. By 1951 that number had increased to more than 900. Holcomb had always had some difficulty in delegating responsibility. That may have been due to the fact that Holcomb was accustomed to the role of the pastor and having a small staff to supervise. Board employees under Holcomb still remember seeing him sitting at his desk day after day signing all the checks of the Board! Whatever

Opposite page, top: Holcomb speaking at dedication of Glorieta building, 1954

Opposite page, center: Pioneer Week

Opposite page, bottom: Glorieta train station

Above and right: Later construction at Glorieta

Leonard E. Wedel

that act represented, it did not symbolize efficiency! So in 1951 the Personnel Department of the Board was established with Leonard E. Wedel as secretary.

Older ministries of the Board were continued and, in most instances, expanded during the Holcomb era. All of these cannot be mentioned, but a few deserve emphasis. One is the Dargan-Carver Library. E. C. Dargan, who had served as editorial secretary of the Board from 1917 until 1927, was keenly aware of the need for library resources for the editors, writers, and field workers of the Board. At his death, Dargan's personal library became the nucleus of a reference library to

Dargan Memorial Library in 1940

Contemporary partial view of the Dargan-Carver Library

meet this need. The Dargan Memorial Library was formally established at the Board in 1933 with Agnes K. Holmes in charge.

In 1951 the Board provided space and facilities for the recently established Historical Commission of the SBC. Two years later, in 1953, the Dargan Library was merged with the collection of the Historical Commission. The library was renamed the Dargan-Carver Library in honor of Dargan and W. O. Carver, a professor at Southern Seminary and long-time leader in Baptist history interests among Southern Baptists. Helen Conger had become librarian of the Dargan Library in 1947, and she continued as librarian when Dargan-Carver came into existence. This library has become a major resource for the staff of the Board, but it also serves as a major international center for research in Baptist history.

Another ministry, revised and extended under Holcomb, was the work of the Baptist Book Stores. I. J. Van Ness began a cooperative Book Store ministry with state Baptist conventions in 1925. When Holcomb arrived at the Board, seventeen Baptist Book Stores were jointly operated by the Board and various state conventions. Financial and other problems plagued a number of these stores. In 1936 the Board announced the following policy to the Convention:

> Because the Sunday School Board has such a large amount invested in the book stores, it was thought wise to offer to sell its interests in the various stores to such State Boards as desired to buy, or to purchase their interest, if they preferred to sell.[20]

Forty-four Baptist Book Stores were in operation by the end of Holcomb's tenure at the Board. All forty-four were owned and operated solely by the Sunday School Board.

During the administration of I. J. Van Ness the Board hired its first art employee. Herman F. Burns began serving as staff artist in the Editorial Department in 1928. For ten years Burns was a one-man staff, and cover design was the major art concern of the Board. In 1943, under Holcomb, the Board established the Art Department as a vital part of its operation. At Holcomb's retirement the art ministry of the Board had grown "from one artist in a cubby hole to a department of thirteen consecrated and professionally trained people."[21]

Ridgecrest Baptist Assembly became a

Howard P. Colson and Robert L. Jones, artist, ca. 1945

Top: Herman Burns, Charles Miller, and William J. Fallis

Center: Artist, ca. 1956

Bottom: Art Department, ca. 1959

growing influence in Southern Baptist life during the Holcomb years. Although the Board had operated Ridgecrest since 1928, the conference center property had been retained by the SBC. In 1944 title to the Ridgecrest property was transferred to the Board, and the Board assumed "all obligations implicit in this ownership." Perry Morgan, Robert Guy, and Willard K. Weeks administered the assembly while Holcomb was executive-secretary at the Board.

Expansion in other areas continued. In

Pritchell Hall at Ridgecrest, ca. 1955

1941 the Department of Student Work began promoting Religious Focus weeks, a highly successful campus ministry which challenged collegians with the claims of Christianity. In 1944 the Board provided needed encouragement in the development of student ministry at the state convention level by offering to pay one-fourth of the salary of a state student secretary for a period of three years. The Department of Church Architecture was reestablished and strengthened in 1940 after having been discontinued in 1936.

Above: J. O. Williams, Holcomb, Mrs. Willie J. Holcomb, and Harold E. Ingraham

Left: Tower Building under construction

Above: Leonard Wedel, Charles Treadway, and Holcomb

Behind all of these programs of service to Southern Baptists was an army of people. Holcomb's motto had been "the combined judgment and concerted action of all." He had known the support of some extremely talented people at the Board. J. N. Barnette and N. R. Drummond were among his closest personal friends. Barnette, a layman, worked at the Board for thirty years and may have provided the inspiration for the Five-Year Program. He served as head of the Sunday School Department from 1943 until 1957. Drummond's association with Holcomb probably reached back to Holcomb's years in Columbia, Mississippi, where Drummond was a teacher and superintendent of schools. A quiet man, he had served as assistant pastor under Holcomb at Oklahoma City. Holcomb

brought Drummond to the Board in 1936, shortly after Holcomb himself became associated with the Board.

P. E. Burroughs, Hight C Moore, J. O. Williams, H. E. Ingraham, and W. R. White all served in leading positions at the Board. B. B. McKinney and W. Hines Sims spearheaded the music ministry. John L. Hill served as book editor from 1922 until 1949 and was succeeded in the latter year by William J. Fallis, who had a long and distinguished career in that capacity. G. Kearnie Keegan followed Frank H. Leavell as secretary of the Student Department.

W. R. White had left the presidency of Hardin-Simmons University in 1943 to assume an important post at the Board as secretary of the Division of Editorial Service.

When he resigned two years later to return to the pastorate, White was succeeded by Clifton J. Allen, who became one of the significant influences in Christian education among Southern Baptists for the next twenty-five years. Allen had been at the Board since 1937. Upon leaving the Board, W. R. White provided a glowing tribute to his successor:

> I have known Dr. Allen very intimately as my associate. No one has ever grown on me so rapidly. He is a well-informed student of the Word of God and the thought life of today. He is splendidly prepared in his academic and seminary background. Dr. Allen believes the Word of God with all his heart. He is conservative on the great fundamentals, yet is abreast of the times and liberal in techniques. He is both as narrow and as broad as the truth. He had a profound conviction as to Baptist distinctives.[22]

Allen, in his long years of service to the Board and Southern Baptists, fulfilled that tribute.

In addition to those already mentioned, other persons appeared whose names were to become significant in the life of the Board: A. V. Washburn, Jr., J. P. Edmunds, Joe W. Burton, Ina S. Lambdin, Sibley C. Burnett, Charles Treadway, Annie Ward Byrd, Josephine Pile, and Porter Routh. The progress of the Sunday School Board under Holcomb can never be written in terms of "the great man theory"—and certainly not as the "single great man theory." Holcomb was not alone, and he knew it. While social and cultural factors of the postwar years facilitated the ministry of the Board, the "combined judgment and concerted action of all" the associates of Holcomb constituted no small factor either. Together they had attempted to reach "the last church."

When Holcomb retired in 1953, the Sunday School Board had become a "giant" in Southern Baptist life. J. M. Frost would have never believed it! While the pastoral touch so characteristic of Holcomb was still needed, more was demanded of the next executive-secretary. He had to be an efficient administrator and a skilled businessman, as well as a leader, pastor, and "knower" of things Southern Baptist. James L. Sullivan appeared to guide the Board through the rest of the religious fifties, the turbulent sixties, and the first half of the seventies in Southern Baptist life.

Notes

1. Luther Holcomb, "The Faith of My Father" (*The Quarterly Review*, October-December, 1974), p. 5.
2. Clifton J. Allen, "Dr. T. L. Holcomb: A Good Man," an unpublished address in the Holcomb files at Dargan-Carver Library.
3. Holcomb recounts this incident in his last report to the Convention. See SBC *Annual*, 1953, p. 254.
4. Luther Holcomb, "The Faith of My Father," p. 8.
5. James L. Sullivan, "T. L. Holcomb—Denominational Statesman," an unpublished address in the Holcomb files at Dargan-Carver Library.
6. Ibid.
7. P. E. Burroughs, *Fifty Fruitful Years*, p. 257.
8. As cited in Clifton J. Allen.
9. Luther Holcomb, "The Faith of My Father," p. 5.
10. Porter Routh, "Personally" (*The Baptist Program*, December 1972), p. 9.
11. Burroughs, *Fifty Fruitful Years*, p. 265.
12. As quoted in SBC *Annual*, 1936, p. 284.
13. Burroughs, *Fifty Fruitful Years*, p. 270.
14. SBC *Annual*, 1941, p. 334.
15. SBC *Annual*, 1945, p. 311.
16. For a list of some of these hymn books, see Burroughs, *Fifty Fruitful Years*, p. 261.
17. Luther Holcomb, "The Faith of My Father," p. 7.
18. SBC *Annual*, 1937, p. 312.
19. These and other developments at the Board during the Holcomb years are outlined in "18 Years of Progress, 1935-1953," a pamphlet published by the Board at Holcomb's retirement.
20. SBC *Annual*, 1936, p. 266.
21. "18 Years of Progress, 1935-1953," p. 9.
22. SBC *Annual*, 1945, pp. 304-305.

James Lenox Sullivan

5 James L. Sullivan "Neither to the Right Nor the Left"

James L. Sullivan is a beans and cornbread denominational philosopher from Sullivan's Hollow, Mississippi. One word, more than any other, characterized his philosophy and leadership as executive secretary-treasurer of the Sunday School Board from 1953 until 1975. The word for Sullivan and the Sullivan years at the Board was "balance."

Balance! Middle! Center! He taught it in seminars, preached it in pulpits, wrote it in books, drew it on napkins in the cafeteria as well as chalkboards in conference rooms, led with it as a denominational executive, demonstrated it with statistics, exemplified it in his living, and repeated it and repeated it and repeated it! In his very first report to the Southern Baptist Convention, he said, "As the Sunday School Board continues to grow, it is my prayer and determined hope . . . that it will never veer from the truth either to the right or to the left."[1]

Near the end of his ministry at the Board, he sounded the same note, warning Southern Baptists of theological extremes: "We must take a *solid middle* conservative stance."[2] Speaking of the ministry of the Sunday School Board in the life of the Convention, he said that the Board "serves as a balance wheel of the denomination."[3] The course he followed at the Board was "one of philosophy," and he spelled out that philosophy:

> Under our polity any church can veto any decision made by the Board or denomination. If we ever move too fast or too far, or veer to the right or the left unduly, churches that wish to do so can reject our materials, refuse our programs, and move in any direction they choose. We have no recourse. When such happens, school is out for us. We have lost our opportunity to serve them ever unless of their own volition they choose to return to the use of our materials.[4]

His storytelling kind of philosophical approach could not stay away from imageries of balance. The captain must maintain balance so the ship will not capsize.[5] And the administrator must stand at the fulcrum of the seesaw.[6]

To study Sullivan and his administration is to observe a mile-high tightrope walker. Danger is to either side, as he often said. And so he tried to balance everything he saw, touched, or thought!

fundamentalism	and	liberalism
tradition	and	relevance
evangelism	and	social action
youth's carelessness	and	age's caution
compassion for people	and	reverence for God
delegated authority	and	democratic processes
the practical	and	the abstract
Stamps Baxter	and	Brahms
pipe organs	and	guitars
freedom	and	responsibility
local church autonomy	and	denominational connectionalism
unity	and	diversity
the Board as business	and	the Board as ministry

Name a thesis. Sullivan provides an antithesis so as to get a synthesis.

No one knew better than Sullivan, however, that the mediator is in the most difficult position of all. Through firsthand experience

73

he was keenly aware that "there is peril in operating in the middle." Sobriety and a level head are necessary for the person in the middle. So he never forgot the advice the country preacher in Kentucky gave him when he became the Board's chief executive. Horseflies will bite the finest thoroughbred, said the Kentucky parson. And while the bites hurt, they won't kill the horse unless he loses his head. Then he may run off and break his neck! Sullivan also remembered his father's philosophy: "Son, you are more apt to get bitten by a snake when you are running from a bull than any other time. So always watch both ways."

But for Sullivan, looking both ways was never a matter of cowardice or being without convictions. It was a matter of principle. It was a philosophy inherent in Christian servanthood, mandated by administrative leadership, dictated by the times.

Sullivan had a sense of heritage. He knew well his institution's history. He knew that the Sunday School Board had always existed at the eye of the storm, experiencing crisis after crisis throughout its history. What he never said, but also doubtless knew, was that not one of his predecessors, not even J. M. Frost, had to guide the ship in such turbulence as did he.

Sullivan played football in college. A linebacker on defense, he was a blocking-back on offense. He was always the man in the middle! Not a neat or safe place to be! In a very real sense every leader of the Board has had to play that position. But no one of them was more in this agonizing middle than Sullivan during his twenty-two years as executive-secretary. What prepares one for that pain and privilege? Where had the man come from, and what had conditioned him for the middle? And what does one do in the middle?

Like Holcomb before him and Cothen after him, Sullivan came from Mississippi. But let him say it:

> God is good. He let me be born and bred at the buckle of the Bible Belt. The church was an integral part of our lives. Its people were our best friends. From earliest childhood we were taught to love books and "learning," to quest for knowledge, and to rejoice when we discovered a new truth. It was the Bible, however, that held a special place in our home and lives as the Book among books. We were taught to study its contents with devotion because it was a unique book given by God for a special purpose and would reveal truths we could never discover otherwise. We were taught to search for its deeper meanings, respect truth from heaven, and apply its teachings to our daily lives.[7]

So Sullivan came from the Bible Belt, and he came with a Bible. The church was central in his life from his earliest days. He made his first speech, led in his first public prayer, and presided over his first business meeting in a Baptist Training Union.

Valedictorian of the 1928 class at Tylertown High School, Sullivan graduated from Mississippi College with distinction in 1932. When as a high school youngster he announced his intention to enter the ministry, he planned to teach in a Bible college. A student pastorate during seminary days made a pastor out of him, though his ministry at the Sunday School Board would, in a sense, return him to a teaching role.

Beginning in 1932 with the Mount Moriah Baptist Church in Boston, Kentucky, Sullivan served six other Baptist churches. His pastoral experience introduced him to the broad range of Southern Baptist church life—the rural, the small town, the college church, and the large city church. He served in the states of Kentucky, Tennessee, Mississippi, and Texas, concluding his pastoral ministry in the First Baptist Church of Abilene, Texas. In churches of all sizes and on both sides of the Mississippi River, he learned the depth and breadth of diversity in Southern Baptist life. It was a diversity which he honored and which he sought to serve at the Sunday School Board. It was also a diversity which goes far in explaining his desire to be in the center of Southern Baptists. In an autobiographical statement he indicated what his years as a Baptist pastor had taught him:

> These years in the pastorate taught me how to love people, work with people,

relate to organizations, plan objectives, deal with opposition, make difficult decisions, stand by those decisions even under stress, and still keep a good relationship with the masses so that no one would be personally offended by what we were seeking to do.[8]

While a pastor, Sullivan had immersed himself in denominational life. A moderator of two Baptist associations, he had served also as the president of a state Training Union Convention and president of a state Baptist convention. He was a member of the board of trustees of three colleges, one seminary, and two hospitals. While pastor at Belmont Heights Baptist Church in Nashville, he was a member of the board of trustees of the Sunday School Board from 1947 until 1950. In that capacity he got an inside look at the institution he would lead only three years later. Sullivan brought to the Board as much denominational know-how as any of those who went before him. He knew *how* Southern Baptists functioned—and *why*.

When he left Abilene, some asked him why he was leaving the ministry. He responded by saying that he was only moving from spiritual retailing (the pastorate) to spiritual wholesaling (the Board). His terminology revealed something about the man. While he brought to the Board the same kind of pastoral concern which characterized Frost, Bell, Van Ness, and Holcomb, he also brought a high degree of business and administrative competence. To some extent this was a competence instinctive to Sullivan's nature. To some extent he had learned from experience. This competence was challenged as he found himself in the middle of some of the toughest years and thorniest problems of any Board leader.

In the Middle of Social Turbulence

One year after Sullivan assumed the leadership of the Sunday School Board, the Supreme Court of the United States issued the landmark decision on public school desegregation. In a very real sense the trauma of the 1960s began in 1954. It lasted until the early 1970s and the ending of the war in Vietnam.

For the Sunday School Board these were the Sullivan years. Nationally they were years of racial violence, of political assassinations, of protest on college campuses, and of the most controversial war America had ever known. The atmosphere was charged with extremes. Charges and countercharges prevailed. Anti-institutionalism dominated both political and religious life. It was not a good time to be the head of any organization or institution.

Sullivan went to the Board in June 1953 to perform tasks for the denomination which he thought he could launch immediately. But he found "a different world emerging only a matter of months" after his arrival. Social upheaval in the nation dictated, to some extent, what could and could not be done. Basic to the social upheaval was race relations. And no section of the nation was more affected than the South—the geographical area where Southern Baptist strength was greatest.

As the head of the Sunday School Board, which was owned and operated by a conservative, white denomination in the South, Sullivan found himself in the middle of the racial conflict on several occasions. He sought to steer the Board between a policy of social activism on the one hand and a reactionary policy which sanctioned the status quo on the other. Writing of the publication policy of the Board during these difficult years, Sullivan said: "Our publications did not back away from their historic stand that we should be Christian at all times to all races regardless of circumstances. While we never promoted integration per se, we always pushed for a Christian attitude toward all people."[9] The result was that the Board angered both the reactionaries and the activists. Fire came from both sides.

The precarious position of the Board was reflected in two controversies. In the "Baldwin Controversy" the attack came from the right. A book by a black author, James Baldwin, was listed in the bibliography of a Training Union publication for youth in July 1964 An extremist group reproduced some Training Union cover jackets and inserted pages, filled with vulgarities, from the Baldwin book. This material was then mailed to Southern Baptist churches. Outrage followed, though the

Board later admitted the listing of the book to be an "error."[10]

A few years later the *"Becoming* Controversy" erupted. *Becoming* was a publication for fourteen-year-old pupils. As editor-in-chief of all Board publications, Sullivan directed that one issue be withheld so revisions could be made. The revisions had to do with a picture portraying one black male and two white female college students in conference in a college library and some written material which Sullivan considered inflammatory. On this occasion the criticism came from those who thought Sullivan and the Board were unduly cautious and conservative in the area of race relations. After the revisions of the written material were made, Sullivan authorized the same lesson on the same subject to run in the subsequent edition. Also, since the publication was for fourteen-year-olds, he suggested that the picture should show fourteen- and fifteen-year-old black and white boys and girls seated around a table. Such explanations did not silence critics, however.

Some saw the work of the Board in the area of race relations as too timid and indirect. Others viewed the Board as too aggressive and direct. In reflecting upon these difficult

Opposite page: (front row) W. D. Kendall and Clifton J. Allen; (back row) Odell Crowe, Noble Van Ness, William J. Fallis, and Herman Burns

Above: J. M. Crowe

years and the position of the Board, Sullivan echoed his philosophy of balance. He said, "The Sunday School Board was thrown into the dilemma of charting its course so as to help the churches maintain balance and make judgments that were right and lasting, that they would not regret later."[11]

In the Middle of Institutional Needs

Van Ness was an educator primarily concerned with the internal operations of the Board. Holcomb was a promoter primarily concerned with the external ministry of the Board. Psychologically and administratively Sullivan stood between Van Ness and Holcomb and their respective emphases. In a very real sense, Sullivan balanced and combined Van Ness and Holcomb. He sought to balance the internal needs of the Board with the external responsibilities of the Board. He viewed the Board as both educator and evangelist, as both business enterprise and spiritual minis-

try. He wanted to coordinate the work of the Board on the inside and implement the work of the Board on the outside. That is, however, probably too much to expect of any one person.

So while Sullivan struck a better balance than any of his predecessors, the weight of his work came down on the internal organization of the Sunday School Board without neglecting the external ministry of the Board. When Sullivan was elected as executive-secretary, the Board needed an administrator with a pastoral heart who understood the business dimension of the Board. Holcomb had promoted. The times now demanded internal consolidation, coordination, and efficiency. Sullivan was thrust, therefore, into the role of a "corporate manager." He had to become a "ministerial businessman."

Upon relinquishing the leadership to Sullivan, Holcomb himself told Sullivan that the Board needed immediate internal reorganization. And while Sullivan had intended to spend his first year studying and evaluating the Board, he discovered that the situation woud not allow the luxury of delay. Clifton Allen correctly said that the Board had begun with a mission but without an organization. The work of the Board had evolved an organization which had grown like Topsy over the years. Sullivan had to give his energies to perfecting the burgeoning system which served the churches.

He began immediately. In the June meeting of 1953 the Board appointed a "Plans and Policies Committee" to work with Sullivan to reorganize the internal operations. Securing the counsel of professional management consultants, the Board adopted a report in June 1954 which enlarged the administrative organization, redefined divisions, and realigned departments of the Board. Four staff positions became a basic part of the executive office. J. M. Crowe assumed the office of administrative assistant to the executive-secretary, Clifton J. Allen the office of editorial secretary, and Leonard E. Wedel the office of personnel manager. Norris Gilliam became the contracts and investment counselor.

In the reorganization, the Board created four divisions to replace the three previous

77

W. L. Howse

R. L. Middleton

H. E. Ingraham

Keith Von Hagen

78

divisions. W. L. Howse, a professor of religious education at Southwestern Seminary, became head of the Education Division. Harold E. Ingraham, a Board mainstay for years, directed the Service Division. Robert L. Middleton headed the Business Division and Keith C. Von Hagen the Merchandise and Sales Division.

From 1953 until 1958 a "quiet revolution," as Robert A. Baker called it, occurred at the Board. In his 1958 report to the Convention, Sullivan summarized the first five years of his administration with three words: "evaluation, adjustment, and undergirding." "These tedious processes," he said, "have required much time for long-range planning, detailed analysis, and organizational realignment."[12] The 1954 reorganization was the first but not the last under Sullivan.

Sullivan was clear about the spiritual ministry of the Board. The purpose of the Board was "to help God's people know God's Book" so they "might practice it diligently and teach it fervently."[13] He also recognized, however, that the Board was a business which demanded efficiency in operation. A new vocabulary came into vogue at the Board. Words such as "managers," "accountability," "marketing," "delegation," "coordination," and "productivity" characterized the Sullivan years.

An administrator unlike any the Board had known was at work. And while Southern Baptists generally would feel the results only indirectly, the employees of the Board reaped direct benefits. Job descriptions, for example, were utilized. An employee credit union was formed. A salary structure based upon equitable principles was initiated. People doing comparable work received the same pay. Remembering the reaction to this policy, Sullivan said, "We never received any complaints when the blacks began receiving the same pay as the whites when they did the same work. Oddly enough, we almost had a revolution when we started paying the women as much as the men under the same circumstances."[14]

Sullivan modernized the operation of the Sunday School Board in multiple ways. His contribution to this aspect of the Board's life was reflected in a scroll given to him by the trustees of the Board in 1974 at the Southern Baptist Convention. On behalf of the thirty thousand churches cooperating with the SBC, the trustees expressed appreciation to Sullivan "for the positively Christian business insight applied to the mammoth business operations of the Board, providing excellence in materials at minimum cost to our churches."

As always, the work of the Board under Sullivan was never a one-person show. At the time of his retirement in February 1975, Sullivan had over fourteen hundred employees at the Board. All were important. None had been more important, however, than J. M. Crowe. He had served as an associate minister with Sullivan at First Baptist Church in Abilene, Texas. Coming to the Board with Sullivan, Crowe served in the various positions of administrative assistant to the executive-secretary, associate executive-secretary, and finally executive vice-president of the Board.

Sullivan was the architect of new plans and policies of the Board. Crowe was the contractor who translated those plans into reality on a daily basis. Always in a supporting role, Crowe was Sullivan's right-hand man during Sullivan's tenure at the Board. They retired at the same time.

Physical expansion was a major feature of the Board under Sullivan's guidance. Approximately fifty buildings were constructed, replaced, or renovated. Almost all of the Glorieta Conference Center was constructed. Much of Ridgecrest was rebuilt. In Nashville a much-needed Operations Building was built. Baptist Book Store buildings were developed throughout the country. In spite of the high cost of such expansion, the buildings were paid for as they progressed. Sullivan said that "the building of all of these structures, although exceedingly expensive, was one of the easiest areas in which I have operated."[15]

If physical construction was an easy task, program correlation was one of Sullivan's most difficult functions. He sought not only to correlate the inner workings of the Board but also to coordinate the ministry of the Board with other denominational agencies. One of the best examples of the latter was the development of the Life and Work Curriculum. Introduced in 1966, this alternate curriculum

Top: Sullivan speaking at the laying of the cornerstone of the Operations Building in 1959

Bottom: Ridgecrest Baptist Conference Center

Opposite page, top: The Shipping Building was renovated in 1960 and renamed the North Wing.

Center left: Baptist Book Store in Houston, Texas

Lower left: Pritchell Hall at Ridgecrest

Middle and lower right: Holcomb Auditorium at Glorieta

BAPTIST BOOK STORE

RIDGECREST

for adults and young people was a joint effort of the Sunday School, Training Union, and Church Music departments of the Board in cooperation with the Woman's Missionary Union and the Brotherhood Commission. It represented an effort at correlation of study materials, but it also symbolized the sensitivity of the Board to the diverse needs in Southern Baptist churches.

As an administrator, Sullivan honed the organization for efficiency, constructed necessary physical facilities, and coordinated the ministry of the Board. That was the "inside" work. By no means, however, was the "outside" work overlooked. Shortly after Sullivan arrived in Nashville, the Sunday School Board launched a campaign to enroll one million additional people in Southern Baptist Sunday schools in 1954. The campaign, known as "A Million More in '54," was the brainchild of J. N. Barnette. Using the principles of Arthur Flake, Barnette guided the campaign. While the effort reached only 600,000 people, it acted as a catalyst in Southern Baptist Sunday School growth. Southern Baptists could soon boast of having the largest Sunday School movement in the world.

The Board sponsored or cooperated in other outreach campaigns such as "the 30,000 Movement"[16] of 1959-64, "Operation Enlargement-Evangelism"[17] of the early 1960s, and "Adult Thrust"[18] of 1964. All such attempts, however, could not forestall the slowing trends that had hit most denominations a decade earlier. In 1963 Sullivan reported to the Convention that "Our growth rate has not been sufficiently large to be satisfactory because we have not reached enough people for Bible study and membership training." He added, "This is our major burden."[19] That burden continued throughout the sixties. By 1970 an actual decline in enrollment in both Sunday School and Training Union appeared as compared to 1969. In 1971 the Board reported a decrease in circulation of church literature.

What had happened? For one thing, the 1960s constituted an era of negativism in matters of religion. Two Southern Baptists had gone through some theological controversy,

and the Board had felt a negative impact from the polarization. Three, independent publishers intensified efforts to appeal to Southern Baptists. Four, for a number of reasons, denominational loyalty began to slip as a prime Southern Baptist characteristic. These and other factors caused a decline in enrollment in church educational programs and the decrease in the Sunday School Board's literature circulation.

This slowdown should not obscure the fact that an overall growth occurred from 1953 to 1975. Enrollment in Sunday School increased from 5,759,128 to 7,182,550; Vacation Bible School from 2,108,370 to 3,239,973; and Church Training from 1,849,544 to 1,949,640. Total receipts at the Board had gone from $12,696,200 to $47,844,000.

Sullivan never wanted promotion to get ahead of education. He admitted that if he "had been a pushy type of person and had assumed the autocratic role of a hard driver," more could have been accomplished in enrollment and enlistment. His conviction, however, was that sustained growth did not come through such methods. He sought "to pace the development and promotion of programs at the Sunday School Board in such a way that the churches would be strengthened on a permanent basis."[20] Even if the Board had been highly promotional during the Sullivan era, the growth the Board had known in the forties and early fifties would probably not have been matched. The sixties were different!

New programs which provided a ministry to Southern Baptists emerged during these years. The Board launched a program of church-related vocational guidance, established the Church Recreation Department, and opened the Church Program Training Center, designed to offer short-term educational opportunities. The two most massive publication projects in the history of the Board were completed during this period also. These two were the *Encyclopedia of Southern Baptists* and *The Broadman Bible Commentary*. Existing programs were enlarged and strengthened. Serving effectively the churches of the SBC remained the objective and goal of the Board.

In the Middle of Denominational Tensions

Because of its involvement in periodical and book publication, the Sunday School Board is one of the most public and vulnerable of all Southern Baptist agencies. Complicating the task of the Board has been the great diversity in Southern Baptist life. Just as a pastor cannot please all the members of a large congregation, the Board has not had unanimous approval from the millions of Southern Baptist church members and the thousands of Southern Baptist churches. During the 1960s theological and social rifts in the denomination added unexpected stress to the work of the Board.

One denominational conflict which affected the Board was the "Elliott Controversy." In July 1961 Broadman Press released *The Message of Genesis,* a book by Ralph Elliott, professor of Old Testament at Midwestern Baptist Theological Seminary. Criticism of Elliott's biblical interpretation came quickly and with intensity. Utilizing the historical-critical approach to biblical study, he stressed that Genesis 1—11 deals with theological fact, not day-by-day physical history.

Elliott was not the only one under criticism, however. Critics also attacked Broadman Press, the general book publishing arm of the Sunday School Board, for publishing the book. When the SBC met in San Francisco in June 1962, a messenger to the Convention presented a motion calling on "the Sunday School Board to cease publishing and to recall from all distribution channels, the book, *The Message of Genesis,* by Dr. Ralph Elliott."[21] The motion was defeated, but the Board was squarely in the middle of the debate.

While seeking to provide literature for Sunday School pupils and teachers, the Board also felt a responsibility to publish books for teaching purposes in theological seminaries. After the book created such a furor in the denomination, however, Sullivan made an administrative decision that the Board would not reprint Elliott's book. The full Board confirmed Sullivan's decision. That decision elicited criticism, as did the publication of the book.

The Elliott controversy left a legacy of suspicion among some Southern Baptists toward both the SBC-owned seminaries and the Sunday School Board. That suspicion solidified at the end of the decade in another theological debate—the "Broadman Bible Commentary" Controversy. Conceived in 1957, approved by the Sunday School Board in 1961, and not finally concluded until 1973, *The Broadman Bible Commentary* is a twelve-volume set of commentaries which was "designed for those who feel a need for a more thoughtful type of work, probing in depth into the truths of God's Word."[22]

As the title indicates, the commentary came from Broadman Press. Eventually, every volume of the commentary would be criticized, but the major objections centered on volume 1 and the exposition of the book of Genesis which was released in October 1969. In June 1970 the SBC met in Denver for what some believed to be the noisiest convention ever. The Convention, by an overwhelming vote, adopted the following motion: "that because the new *The Broadman Commentary* is out of keeping with the beliefs of the vast majority of Southern Baptist pastors and people this convention requests the Sunday School Board to withdraw volume 1 from further distribution and that it be rewritten with due consideration of the conservative viewpoint."[23]

In keeping with what they thought to be the directive of the Denver Convention, the trustees of the Board asked the authors of volume 1 to rewrite some of the material "with due consideration of the conservative viewpoint." Guidelines for rewriting the material were worked out between the Board and the authors. All such agreements were for naught, however. When the SBC met in 1971 in St. Louis, an adopted motion called for the dismissal of the authors of volume 1.

Following the St. Louis Convention, the trustees of the Board secured Clyde T. Francisco to write the commentary on Genesis in the revised edition of volume 1. The revised edition was released in 1973 without significant reaction.

James L. Sullivan had defended the un-

Opposite page, left: Chester Ellis retired in 1971 after 46 years at the Board.

Opposite page, right: Sullivan poses with copies of the book *John's Witness to Jesus,* which he authored.

Below left: Sullivan and C. C. Warren with W. L. Howse and A. V. Washburn

Below right: Sullivan addresses trustees

Bottom left: Castro Parker and Joe Burton

Bottom right: Philip and Miriam Harris and J. E. and Ina Lambdin

revised edition of volume 1 on two grounds. One, he indicated that no book produced by Broadman Press was considered to be the official position of the Southern Baptist Convention. Two, he insisted that the Board produced books for various segments of Southern Baptists. So while the Board acknowledged the diversity of needs within Southern Baptist life and sincerely wanted to minister to those needs, Convention action had made that task exceedingly difficult for the Board. The Board, therefore, found itself where it had been throughout much of its life—in the middle of an exceedingly diverse denomination.

Compounding this problem for the Board, and all other SBC agencies, is the relationship between the trustee system of governing the agencies and the ultimate control of the SBC over those agencies. The Convention elects trustees to administer the affairs of the Board. But when messengers to the SBC have taken matters in their own hands and have sought to direct the operations of the Board from the floor of the Convention, the administration of the Board is complicated and the trustee system is destroyed. Sullivan had constantly warned Southern Baptists of the danger of overcentralization in denominational affairs. He has also likewise cautioned against the

anarchy that can result from bypassing the trustee system of directing the internal affairs of the denomination's agencies. With typical balance, he has called for delegation without centralization.[24]

Progress in the Midst of Problems

While the Board faced problems during the tumultuous sixties, it also experienced progress. The very fact that the Board entered the early seventies with a forward look reflected the resilience and health of the institution. Humor had often helped relieve the pressure of controversy. The Board received one letter containing the following request. ''Please tell me what the Bible teaches. Limit contents to half a page.'' Another request, more impossible to understand and to satisfy, said, ''Please send me the Sunday School Board without obligation. Sincerely yours.'' One person ordered a book entitled *A Fat Man Speaks*. The Board had never produced a book by that title and did not know how to respond. A clerk in the Baptist Book Store guessed that the person really wanted *Broadman Comments!*

By the time James L. Sullivan retired as the leader of the Board, the institution had been firmly established as the world's largest religious publishing agency. It had been placed on sound financial management principles, reflecting the business part of the life of the Board. It had been structured for efficiency in its organizational capacity. It had continued to contribute to the sense of denominational identity among Southern Baptists by encouraging the coordination of ministries among denominational agencies. And even in the face of some vocal independent movements, the Board continued to function effectively as a denominationalizer of local churches, district associations, and state Baptist conventions.

Beyond the business, organizational, and denominational aspects, the Board never forgot that its ultimate purpose was to impress on the lives of human beings the claims and the gospel of Jesus Christ. The philosopher from Sullivan's Hollow was speaking of the institution he led for over twenty-one years when he wrote:

It must be consciously spiritual in every plan and must keep before its workers the spiritual nature of the institution and the spiritual impact it is having upon the people and the nation. Never can the Sunday School Board follow a rigid role of a strict business operation, giving attention to cold organizational principles, methodology, or finances. These are important, but the really important thing is the ultimate spiritual impact. The work we do affects spiritual lives and homes of the people whom we serve by the millions.[25]

At the center of this spiritual ministry was the Bible. Sullivan's successor would continue to stress that ''the Bible is the thing'' for the Sunday School Board.

Notes

1. SBC *Annual*, 1954, p. 252.
2. James L. Sullivan, *God Is My Record* (Nashville: Broadman Press, 1974), p. 138. Underlining is mine and for emphasis.
3. Ibid., p. 111.
4. Ibid., p. 98.
5. James L. Sullivan, *Rope of Sand with Strength of Steel* (Nashville: Convention Press, 1974), p. 129.
6. Sullivan, *God Is My Record*, p. 111.
7. Ibid., p. 7.
8. Ibid., p. 97.
9. Ibid., p. 90.
10. SBC *Annual*, 1965, p. 184.
11. Sullivan, *God Is My Record*, p. 123.
12. SBC *Annual*, 1958, p. 249.
13. Ibid.
14. Sullivan, *God Is My Record*, p. 53.
15. Ibid., p. 42.
16. This was a SBC-wide effort to establish thirty thousand new missions or preaching stations between 1959-1964.
17. This was a project sponsored jointly by the Sunday School Board and the Home Mission Board.
18. This was the first step in a Board effort to achieve an enrollment of ten million in Southern Baptist Sunday Schools by 1970.
19. SBC *Annual*, 1963, p. 178.
20. Sullivan, *God Is My Record*, p. 98.
21. SBC *Annual*, 1962, p. 71.
22. James L. Sullivan, ''Memo on Christian Education: The Broadman Bible Commentary,'' *Facts and Trends*, April 1970, p. 2.
23. SBC *Annual*, 1970, p. 63.
24. Sullivan, *Rope of Sand with Strength of Steel*, p. 105.
25. Sullivan, *God Is My Record*, p. 99.

Grady Coulter Cothen

6 Grady C. Cothen "The Bible Is the Thing"

J. M. Frost, at sixty-eight years of age, died in office as the executive leader of the Sunday School Board. I. J. Van Ness retired at age seventy-five, and T. L. Holcomb retired at age seventy. James L. Sullivan, in reflecting upon this trend, vowed that he would do two things in preparing for his retirement from the Board.

First, he announced his intention to retire at age sixty-five. Second, he decided early in his ministry at the Board to assume personal responsibility for effecting a smooth transition between himself and his successor. In order to maintain continuity in operations at the Board during the period of transition, Sullivan wanted his successor to be selected one year before assuming the full weight of responsibilities. The trustees adopted Sullivan's suggestion and named Grady C. Cothen as president-elect of the Board on February 5, 1974.

That was one year prior to Sullivan's retirement date. Cothen came to the Board in May 1974 and spent nine months in orientation and preliminary planning. The transition period provided him an opportunity to visit all state convention offices and to become acquainted with the operations of the Board. He became the sixth executive leader of the Sunday School Board on February 4, 1975.

Cothen brought to the Board more varied experience in denominational administration than any of the men who preceded him. Prior to coming to the Board, Cothen served for five years as president of the New Orleans Baptist Theological Seminary. Before that he had been the president of Oklahoma Baptist University and executive-secretary of the Baptist General Convention of California. His pastoral experience included the White Oak Baptist Church, Chattanooga, Tennessee; Olivet Baptist Church, Oklahoma City, Oklahoma; and First Baptist Church, Birmingham, Alabama.

With the announcement of Cothen's election as president of the Sunday School Board, one state Baptist editor wrote, "The presidency of the Sunday School Board requires the patience of a Job, the wisdom of a Solomon, the dedication of a Paul and then a bit more." With realistic commendation, he added, "Cothen won't match any of these gentlemen but he will come as near to the ideal as any man we know."[1]

Cothen has now served at the Board about six and one-half years. The emphases of the Board under his administration to this point are clear. He outlined the priorities of the Board in his report to the Southern Baptist Convention in June 1975. Following his leadership, the trustees of the Board formally adopted these priorities the next month.

The first priority has been to provide in-depth Bible study for the masses. This reaffirmation of the central role of the Bible in the work of the Board came at a crucial time in the life of Southern Baptists. On the heels of the "Broadman Bible Commentary Controversy," in 1973 a very small but vocal group of Southern Baptists formed an organization called "The Baptist Faith and Message Fellowship." The name came from the confessional statement which the SBC adopted in 1963 following the "Elliott Controversy." Agitating for a strict adherence to the statement related to the Bible which is contained in the confession, this group also began attacking what it perceived as doctrinal impurity among Southern Baptists.

In the face of the accusations, one of Cothen's first public statements as president of the Sunday School Board dealt with the issue of the Bible and the Board. Describing Southern Baptists as "a people of the book," Cothen began by saying:

> Controversy swirls about the nature of the Bible once again. It seems that each generation must discover for itself the nature of God's Word and affirm its faith in it as Holy Scripture. Our time is no different.[2]

He then indicated that the Board would operate within the theological framework of "The Baptist Faith and Message." But he reminded his readers that the Preamble to that confession stated "that the sole authority for faith and practice among Baptists is the Scriptures of the Old and New Testaments."

"Southern Baptists have said it," Cothen continued; "the Bible is the thing." He concluded with a paragraph which contained his personal philosophy and his understanding of the purpose of the Board:

> For me, I have signed the Baptist Faith and Message statement because I believe it. I will not substitute it for the Bible! With clear instructions from the convention through our trustees, I see our task at the Board to be teaching of the Word, not debating about it; helping "bring men to God through Jesus Christ" rather than controversy; helping men toward maturity in the faith more than arguing a point of view.[3]

This statement was so important for Cothen that he reprinted it in the November 1980 issue of *Facts and Trends*.

Rhetoric was not enough, however. So the Board set out to implement the number 1 priority of leading Southern Baptists in a new day of Bible study. That priority had been expressed in several concrete ways. For example, in February 1976, the trustees of the Board approved a new Sunday School curriculum series providing a sequential and systematic study of books of the Bible. Introduced in October 1978 and known as the "Bible Book Series," this new curriculum involved a nine-year study plan to cover all sixty-six books of the Bible.

The new curriculum afforded Southern Baptist churches three choices in Sunday School materials. The Convention Uniform Series and the Life and Work Series had distinctives of their own, but neither constituted the approach of the new curriculum. It immediately claimed about 13 percent of the total Sunday School youth and adult circulation.

Also indicative of the renewed emphasis on Bible study was the development of ACTION, a new approach to enrolling people in the Sunday Schools. This program had been developed by E. S. Anderson while he was pastor of Riverside Baptist Church in Fort Myers, Florida. The Board secured the copyright to the ACTION materials and employed Anderson as a Sunday School consultant in 1975. ACTION consisted of enrolling persons in Sunday School anytime, anywhere the persons agreed to be enrolled; but the plan was most often used in door-to-door surveys. Two thousand churches used the ACTION plan in its first full year of promotion by the Board. During the 1975-76 year, Sunday School enrollment increases were the largest since 1969.

In addition to this attempt to increase existing Sunday Schools, an effort was launched to establish new Sunday Schools. By the end of 1978-79, the goal of establishing three thousand new Sunday Schools in three years had been exceeded. Sunday School work among Southern Baptists, therefore, entered the decade of the eighties with an emphasis on outreach and evangelism.

If the Board was to reach the masses with Bible study, it had to capitalize on television. So in cooperation with the Southern Baptist Radio and Television Commission, the Board initiated a radio-television Bible correspondence course in 1978. The radio-television program is a thirty-minute religious broadcast and is called "At Home with the Bible." Hosted by Frank Pollard, pastor of the First Baptist Church in San Antonio, Texas, the program features singing, interviews, and a ten- to twelve-minute Bible teaching segment.

The audience of the program is invited to write for a free copy of the *Home Bible Study Guide,* a monthly publication including Bible background material and study questions. Supported solely by the Board and contributions from respondents, the program has received national recognition. The National Religious Broadcasters Association gave the Award of Merit for Excellence in Television Programming to the program in 1980.

Two other examples of the priority of Bible teaching at the Board need to be noted. One was the purchase by the Board on May 1, 1979, of the A. J. Holman Company, America's oldest Bible publishing firm. "This gives us—and Southern Baptists in general—a Bible base that we have never had before,"[4] said Cothen. He and Jim Clark, executive vice-president of the Board, believe that this is one of the most significant steps ever taken by the Board. The Board has also accented Bible study with the planned publication of the *Layman's Bible Book Commentary*, a twenty-four-volume work designed, as the title suggests, for the laity.

Shortly after he assumed the leadership of the Board, Grady Cothen wrote that "one of our most urgent needs is to get the Bible to America."[5] In the five years since he wrote that sentence, the Board has planned a new Bible curriculum for Sunday Schools, adopted promotional efforts to enlist people in Bible study, designed a major radio-television program for teaching the Bible, purchased a Bible publishing firm, and begun releasing a Bible commentary for laypeople. Plans are under way for the Board to lead—with other agencies—in a denominational video network and a telecommunication network that will take the Bible's message to America and the world. When he said, "The Bible is the thing," he obviously meant it! It has been the Board's number 1 priority.

The Board's second major priority for the decade of 1975-85 is to "equip the saints." The concern here is to aid Christians who have not matured into the likeness of Christ, and it signals an effort to restore the importance of the Church Training program in local Baptist churches. Two promotional campaigns have begun. One, known as the "New Day for Training," succeeded in forming 528 new Church Training programs in SBC churches in one year.[6] A second, "Build-Up—A Church Training Enrollment Plan," provides for enrolling all church members in discipleship and leadership training.

In response to the Board's priority "to equip the saints," the Church Training Department has developed an innovative approach to training for adults and youth

James W. Clark

which is known as "Equipping Centers." The Equipping Center modules, or courses, are undated materials designed to be used by individuals or groups. These modules are arranged for short-term training and are adaptable to flexible schedules. Developed around the six content areas of evangelism and missions, Christian doctrine, family life, leadership, church and community, and Christian growth, the Equipping Center modules are packaged in boxes. They are reusable and require minimal organization.

An effort "to enrich and support family life" constitutes the third priority which the Board adopted. Thus, a longtime area of ministry for the Board has received new attention during a time when social and cultural forces threaten the security of the family. Symbolizing the importance of this ministry, the trustees of the Board authorized the establishment of the Family Ministry Department in 1975.

The program of the Family Ministry Department is comprehensive in scope. It is "to develop the services and materials acceptable for use by Southern Baptist churches, associations, and state conventions in establishing, conducting, and improving family ministry services of marriage and family enrichment, parent enrichment skills, ministries to single persons, premarriage and remarriage education, and personal and spiritual enrichment of senior adults and leaders of senior adults."[7]

92

New publications have been released to assist in this crucial ministry to families. *Mature Living,* a monthly magazine for senior adults, was begun in 1977 and called for "a rebirth of respect for older persons." Two years later the Board began publishing *Christian Single,* a monthly magazine targeted to never-married, divorced, and widowed adults. Two new quarterly publications, *Living with Children* and *Living with Teenagers,* have been produced to enrich parenting. In addition to the new publications, considerable attention has been given to the promotion of Family Enrichment Conferences. The Board sponsored the first national Family Enrichment Conference in 1975-76 at Glorieta Conference Center with 865 participants.[8]

This focus on the family reflects the Board's desire for relevance within the context of biblical teachings and Christian ministry, as well as support of local church needs in Southern Baptist life.

The fourth and final priority outlined by Cothen and adopted by the Board is "to encourage and aid pastors, church staffs, and their families." Prompted by requests from a number of church and denominational people, the Board implemented a Career Guidance Section in the Church Administration Department in 1976. In fact, the Church Administration Department was reorganized "to obtain greater thrust" for achieving the goal of aiding and encouraging pastors and other church staff members.[9]

The new Career Guidance Section has been involved in four areas of work, some of which have received minimum attention by the SBC in the past. First, an effort has been made to discover those persons called to Christian ministry so as to nurture them throughout their ministry careers. Second, career assessment and consultation has been provided to SBC ministers. Third, a coordinated pastoral support system, including a nationwide clinical counseling/referral network, has been attempted. Fourth, a ministry research service for compiling data on various aspects of the ministry has begun. All of these constitute efforts to strengthen ministers so as to strengthen the church's ministry.

While not directly related to this fourth priority of the Board, a cooperative effort between the Sunday School Board and the Southern Baptist seminaries also suggests the Board's interest in the future ministers of the SBC. In 1978 the Board volunteered to pay the salary of one seminary professor who would serve in a liaison capacity between the theological institutions and the Board and other denominational agencies. Designed to help the Board stay abreast of current academic thought in matters related to the purpose of the Board and also to expose seminary students to the services of the Board, this interagency coordination speaks of the Board's broad interest in denominational life.

The "Cothen Years" continue. And they continue as the "Frost Years" began—with the dedicated support of all of the employees of the Board. One other factor remains crucial to the ministry of the Board within the denomination, however. And that is what James L. Sullivan described as the Board's greatest asset. It is the confidence of the Southern Baptist people.

Notes

1. *The Baptist Standard,* February 27, 1974.
2. *Facts and Trends,* March 1975, p. 2.
3. Ibid.
4. Ibid., July—August 1979, p. 2.
5. Ibid., June 1975.
6. SBC *Annual,* 1979, p. 119.
7. SBC *Annual,* 1978, p. 148.
8. SBC *Annual,* 1977, p. 133.
9. Ibid., p. 131.

Conclusion

"Any evaluation of the Sunday School Board of the Southern Baptist Convention," said Gomer R. Lesch, "must in large measure be an evaluation of its chief executive." As long as one qualifies that judgment with the words "in large measure," it is a correct assessment. The leaders of the Board have certainly stamped the institution with each of their respective personalities and emphases.

Frost dreamed the institution into existence and nursed it through its early years. T. P. Bell served as an apologist for the Board, defending it and guaranteeing its existence. I. J. Van Ness focused on the editorial quality of the Board's publications; he "educated" it. T. L. Holcomb promoted and popularized the ministry of the Board. James L. Sullivan refined the organization, built physical facilities, and introduced sound management principles. Grady Cothen has entered into the heritage with a clear reaffirmation of the centrality of the Bible in the ministry of the Board.

The rhythm of the history of the Board has meant that each of the executives had a particular job to do. Bell did not have to launch the Board; Frost had already done so. Van Ness did not have to fight for the Board's continuing existence; Frost and Bell had already done so. Holcomb did not have to stress publications; Van Ness had already done so. Sullivan did not have to be a promoter; Holcomb had already done so. And Cothen did not have to build up the efficiency of the organization; Sullivan had already done so. Of course, none was free to do just one thing. All dimensions of the Board had to be sustained simultaneously. And as the institution grew in size and importance, the job of leadership grew more complex, troublesome, and challenging.

The times during which each executive served is another important factor in evaluating the Sunday School Board. The social and cultural milieu in which an executive worked was as crucial to the moods of the Board as were the individual gifts and inclinations of the leaders. Holcomb, for example, was burdened with the perplexity of postdepression years, and he was blessed with the religious boom of the postwar years. One condition demanded promotion; the other greatly facilitated it.

The denominational context was as important for the Board as was the more general social environment. During Holcomb's years, the denomination rested in relative tranquillity. This was certainly not the case during the Van Ness and Sullivan years. It is not surprising, therefore, that Van Ness and Sullivan turned their attention to the internal life of the Board, though each did so in different ways. Under Van Ness there was a proliferation of the programs of the Board, while under Sullivan the programs and the organization which implemented them were both refined. Because the Board is a denominational agency, it has been limited and/or liberated to do its work, depending upon the sentiment of the Convention as well as the temperament of the times.

What impact has the Board had on the life of the Southern Baptist Convention? At the 1895 meeting of the SBC in Washington, D.C., W. H. Whitsitt, president and professor of church history at The Southern Baptist Theological Seminary, delivered a "Historical Discourse on the Fiftieth Anniversary of the Southern Baptist Convention." When Whitsitt gave the address, the Sunday School Board was only an infant, four years old. His assessment of the influence of the Board, however, was a glowing one. Whitsitt said:

> The result has transcended the most sanguine anticipations. The Sunday School Board has proved itself a triumphant success, and has done as much as any agency in recent years to excite a sense of pride in our Convention and of confidence in our capacities.[1]

While no student of the history of the Board would claim that the institution has been a "triumphant success" in every way, neither would one dispute Whitsitt's early claim that the Board has done as much as any denominational agency to instill a sense of pride in denominational life.

The Sunday School Board has been a force in denominational life in at least four ways. First, the Board has been an educational force among Southern Baptists. Like Whitsitt, John R. Sampey served as president of Southern Seminary. Also like Whitsitt, he had a profound appreciation for the ministry of the Board. Regarding the fiftieth anniversary history of the Board, Sampey wrote, "The Sunday School Board is our people's university in the teaching of religion."[2]

"Our people," as Sampey affectionately described Southern Baptists, have always been a diverse and assorted lot. They have experienced the notion of the holy in the smallest country church as well as the largest urban church. They have been found among the most highly educated and the most woefully uneducated. They have been rich and they have been poor, and they have responded to different expressions of worship and ministry. And it has been to the diverse lot that the Sunday School Board has been a "university in the teaching of religion." Given the variety of the "students," the mission of the "university" has been—and is—a magnificent impossibility.

At the heart of the curriculum has been the Bible. From the first publication of "Kind Words" to the final page of the twelve-volume *Broadman Bible Commentary,* the Board has attempted to teach Southern Baptists the Word of God. By establishing Sunday Schools, by providing publications for those schools, and by seeking to teach teachers how to teach in those schools, the Board has spearheaded a drive to make the Bible known. No age group has been excluded. In fact, the all-age Sunday School has been the "standard" of the Board.

The educational ministry of the Board has not been limited to the Sunday School emphasis. Through Church Training, the Board has tried to stimulate a study of Christian doctrine, Christian history, and Christian ethics. General leadership development in the churches has been a part of the task of the Church Administration Department. Family life education and music education have also been concerns of the Board.

Ridgecrest and Glorieta Conference Centers have served as vital places of inspiration as well as education. The work of Baptist Book Stores, Broadman Press, and the departments of Church Architecture, Church Library, Church Recreation, and National Student Ministries mirror the educational function of what Sampey called "our people's university."

Second, the Sunday School Board has also been a missionary and evangelistic force. Reflecting upon the origins of the Board, J. M. Frost said that "the Board from the first was missionary in spirit, in didactic power and efficiency."[3] A missionary book, *The Story of Yates the Missionary,* was the first book published by the Board. The Board has sponsored missionary days in the Sunday School and joined in promoting every denominational missions endeavor, including the most recent, "Bold Missions Thrust."

"Flake's Formula" for growing Sunday Schools, "The Five-Year Plan," "A Million More in '54," "ACTION," and many other such programs may have been perceived by some as little more than religious sloganeering. They were at bottom, however, attempts to bring people face to face with God in Jesus Christ. While the Sunday School Board never saw itself as a mission board of the SBC, it has always perceived its task as intensely that of evangelism and missions.

Third, the Board has most certainly been a financial force in the life of the Southern Baptist Convention. In its beginning the Board, as P. E. Burroughs said, was "cradled in poverty." The Board initially was plagued by a poverty of moral and financial support from Southern Baptists. As the Board gradually won the moral support of Southern Baptists, it also began to develop financially.

J. M. Frost was ecstatic when after the first fiscal year the Board had paid all of its bills and had a balance of over one thousand dollars! This, he said, "threw a new light on the future." But it was not simply a new light for the Board's future; it was a light for the future of the Southern Baptist Convention.

Many Southern Baptists do not understand

95

that the Sunday School Board has never received funds from the Cooperative Program. It has *contributed to* rather than *received from* the work of the Cooperative Program. Few, if any, agencies of the SBC which have come into existence since the formation of the Sunday School Board have failed to receive some financial assistance from the Board. This includes the six seminaries, the Annuity Board, the Brotherhood Commission, the Education Commission, and the Executive Committee. Others could be mentioned.

Not only has the Board invested in Southern Baptist life at the national level. It has also been of major importance in helping fund programs such as music, student ministries, Sunday School, Church Training, Church Administration, Church Architecture, Church Library, and Church Recreation at the state convention level. In 1978-79, for example, the Board distributed $1,715,614 to thirty-four state conventions!

Fourth, the Sunday School Board has created denominational unity within the Southern Baptist Convention. This is not to overlook the fact that the Board itself has sometimes been at the center of denominational controversy. Indeed, when J. M. Frost presented the Board's first annual report to the Convention, one earnest and devout leader predicted "that the Sunday School Board would split the Convention wide open."[4]

Rather than splitting the Convention wide open, the Sunday School Board has helped to cement the thirty-five thousand autonomous Southern Baptist churches into a cohesive denomination. But the Board did not set out to accomplish denominational unity. Rather, the wide acceptance of its literature and programs have had the fortunate by-product of achieving this unity. No Southern Baptist institution has done more to denominationalize the Southern Baptist Convention than the Sunday School Board.

Speaking primarily of Basil Manly, Jr., and John A. Broadus, J. M. Frost described the heritage of the Board as "a royal line." Frost was right. And that line has been extended. Through ninety years of history the Sunday School Board has remained "our people's university in the teaching of religion."

Notes

1. SBC *Annual*, 1895, p. 89.
2. In P. E. Burroughs, *Fifty Fruitful Years*, p. 308.
3. J. M. Frost, *The Sunday School Board, Southern Baptist Convention: Its History and Work*, p. 45.
4. Ibid., p. 78.

Serving you for ninety years